A JOURNEY INTO THE LAND OF THE WISE:

Unfolding the Science and Arts of Research

By

Wilmer Joel S. Decano

Dedicated to all my co-teachers
at Exodus Elementary School

INTRODUCTION

I got a dream, a happy dream indeed.

I just saw myself, when I was around eighteen years old with an old friend.

In the dream, we went to a mountain to spend some time to relax after school works.

"Willy, what is our professor's topic again in research?"

"Jolly, it's kinda long. I cannot tell everything."

"Yes I know. But you were writing every words he said."

"Yes in shorthand."

"Well, at least you can share to me."

"Of course. But let us relax. The wind is cold and the sun is warming. It is a perfect afternoon to be silent for a while."

"Ok...But Willy, our professor is somewhat nerdy."

"Why? How do you say so?"

"Well he was talking about that mystical Land of the Wise. There's no such place."

"Who told you?"

"Hmmm…Why do talk like that?   Do you know anything about that land?"

"No. Not me; but my great grandfather."

"Wow, Willy, it's interesting. Please tell me more…"

"Okay, in that land there was no time for things like this – there is no rest, no play, no mediocrity….. everyone were looking for answers to everything."

"And then?"

"They got a book, the Book of the Wise…."

"And what was written there?"

"The most exquisite formula for solving a problem!"

TABLE OF CONTENTS

1

WHAT IS RESEARCH?

Research is defined as careful consideration of study regarding a particular concern or problem using scientific methods.

According to the American sociologist Earl Robert Babbie, "research is a systematic inquiry to describe, explain, predict, and control the observed phenomenon. It involves inductive and deductive methods."

Inductive research methods analyze an observed event, while deductive methods verify the observed event. Inductive approaches are associated with qualitative research, and deductive methods are more commonly associated with quantitative analysis.

Research is conducted with a purpose to:

- Identify potential and new ideas
- Understand existing ideas
- Set pragmatic goals
- Develop productive strategies
- Address challenges
- Put together a plan
- Identify new opportunities

WHAT ARE THE CHARACTERISTICS OF RESEARCH?

1. Good research follows a systematic approach to capture accurate data. Researchers need to practice ethics and a code of conduct while making observations or drawing conclusions.

2. The analysis is based on logical reasoning and involves both inductive and deductive methods.

3. Real-time data and knowledge is derived from actual observations in natural settings.

4. There is an in-depth analysis of all data collected so that there are no anomalies associated with it.

5. It creates a path for generating new questions. Existing data helps create more research opportunities.

6. It is analytical and uses all the available data so that there is no ambiguity in inference.

7. Accuracy is one of the most critical aspects of research. The information must be accurate and correct. For example, laboratories provide a controlled environment to collect data. Accuracy is measured in the instruments used, the calibrations of instruments or tools, and the experiment's final result.

WHAT IS THE PURPOSE OF RESEARCH?

There are three main purposes:

1. **Exploratory:** As the name suggests, researchers conduct exploratory studies to explore a group of questions. The answers and analytics may not offer a conclusion to the perceived problem. It is undertaken to handle new problem areas that haven't been explored before. This exploratory process lays the foundation for more conclusive data collection and analysis.

2. **Descriptive:** It focuses on expanding knowledge on current issues through a process of data collection. Descriptive studies describe the behavior of a sample population. Only one variable is required to conduct the study. The three primary purposes of descriptive studies are describing, explaining, and validating the findings. For example, a study conducted to know if top-level management leaders in the 21st century possess the moral right to receive a considerable sum of money from the company profit.

3. **Explanatory:** Causal or explanatory research is conducted to understand the impact of specific changes in existing standard procedures. Running experiments is the most popular form. For example, a study that is conducted to understand the effect of rebranding on customer loyalty.

Here is a comparative analysis for better understanding:

	Exploratory Research	**Descriptive Research**	**Explanatory Research**
Approach used	Unstructured	Structured	Highly structured
Conducted through	Asking questions	Asking questions	By using hypotheses.
Time	Early stages of decision making	Later stages of decision making	Later stages of decision making

Research begins by asking the right questions and choosing an appropriate method to investigate the problem. After collecting answers to your questions, you can analyze the findings or observations to draw reasonable conclusions.

When it comes to customers and market studies, the more thorough your questions, the better the analysis. You get essential insights into brand perception and product needs by thoroughly collecting customer data through surveys and questionnaires. You can use this data to make smart decisions about your marketing strategies to position your business effectively.

To be able to make sense of your research and get insights faster, it helps to use a research repository as a single source of truth in your organization and to manage your research data in one centralized repository.

TYPES OF RESEARCH

Qualitative methods

Qualitative research is a method that collects data using conversational methods, usually open-ended questions. The responses collected are essentially non-numerical. This method helps a researcher understand what participants think and why they think in a particular way.

Types of qualitative methods include:

1. One-to-one Interview
2. Focus Groups
3. Ethnographic studies
4. Text Analysis
5. Case Study

Quantitative methods

Quantitative methods deal with numbers and measurable forms. It uses a systematic way of investigating events or data. It answers questions to justify relationships with measurable variables to either explain, predict, or control a phenomenon.

Types of quantitative methods include:

1. Survey research
2. Descriptive research
3. Correlational research

Remember, research is only valuable and useful when it is valid, accurate, and reliable. Incorrect results can lead to customer churn and a decrease in sales.

It is essential to ensure that your data is:

- Valid – founded, logical, rigorous, and impartial.

- Accurate – free of errors and including required details.

- Reliable – other people who investigate in the same way can produce similar results.

- Timely – current and collected within an appropriate time frame.

- Complete – includes all the data you need to support your business decisions.

8 TIPS FOR CONDUCTING ACCURATE RESEARCH

1. Identify the main trends and issues, opportunities, and problems you observe. Write a sentence describing each one.

2. Keep track of the frequency with which each of the main findings appears.

3. Make a list of your findings from the most common to the least common.

4. Evaluate a list of the strengths, weaknesses, opportunities, and threats that have been identified in a SWOT analysis.

5. Prepare conclusions and recommendations about your study.

6. Act on your strategies.

7. Look for gaps in the information, and consider doing additional inquiry if necessary.

8. Plan to review the results and consider efficient methods to analyze and dissect results for interpretation.

Review your goals before making any conclusions about your research. Keep in mind how the process you have completed and the data you have gathered help answer your questions. Ask yourself if what your analysis revealed facilitates the identification of your conclusions and recommendations.

2

WHY IS RESEARCH IMPORTANT?

The main purposes of research are to inform action, gather evidence for theories, and contribute to developing knowledge in a field of study. This article discusses the significance of research and the many reasons why it is important for everyone—not just students and scientists.

Understanding that research is important might seem like a no-brainer, but many people avoid it like the plague. Yet, for those who like to learn, whether they are members of a research institution or not, conducting research is not just important—it's imperative.

WHY RESEARCH IS NECESSARY AND VALUABLE IN OUR DAILY LIVES

1. It's a tool for building knowledge and facilitating learning.

2. It's a means to understand issues and increase public awareness.

3. It helps us succeed in business.

4. It allows us to disprove lies and support truths

5. It is a means to find, gauge, and seize opportunities.

6. It promotes a love of and confidence in reading, writing, analyzing, and sharing valuable information.

7. It provides nourishment and exercise for the mind. Conducting research doesn't just arm us with knowledge—it helps teach us how to think.
Maxim Ilyahov via Unsplash; Canva

To explain further…. Note that some materials were constructed with emphasis to business.

1. It's a Tool for Building Knowledge and Facilitating Learning

Research is required not just for students and academics but for all professionals and nonprofessionals alike. It is also important for budding and veteran writers, both offline and online.

For nonprofessionals who value learning, doing research equips them with knowledge about the world and skills to help them survive and improve their lives. Among professionals and scribes, on the other hand, finding an interesting topic to discuss and/or to write about should go beyond personal experience. Determining either what the general public may want to know or what researchers want others to realize or to think about can serve as a reason to do research. Thus, research is an essential component in generating knowledge, and vice-versa.

Knowledge is commonly described as a factual proposition in the mind of an individual. It essentially refers to facts based on objective insights and/or study findings processed by the human brain. It can be acquired through various means, such as reading books and articles, listening to experts, watching documentaries or investigative shows, conducting scientific experiments, and interacting with other people, among others. Facts collected during research can be checked against other sources to ensure their truthfulness and accuracy.

Studies and Articles About the Importance of Research

In his article, "Epistemology," Yale University's David Truncellito (n.d.) identifies three kinds of knowledge: **procedural** (competence or know-how), **acquaintance** (familiarity),
and **propositional** (description of "a fact or a state of affairs").

Brain Research UK (formerly Brain Research Trust), a medical-research charity based in the United Kingdom, acknowledges the importance of research in building knowledge. It sees research as crucial to finding possible cures for diseases and ways to prevent them. Thus, research is necessary to ascertain whether one's ideas are supported by previous studies or if these ideas still need further proof to be considered knowledge.

An example of one such endeavor is a 2016 study conducted by several psychologists to examine how sleep affects memory reactivation. In "Relearn Faster and Retain Longer: Along With Practice, Sleep Makes Perfect," they discovered that "interleaving sleep between learning sessions not only reduced the amount of practice needed by half but also ensured much better long-term retention. Sleeping after learning is definitely a good strategy, but sleeping between two learning sessions is a better strategy." This study supports the fact that both repetition and sleep improve a person's long-term retention of information. Their findings also emphasize how highly important sleep is to healthy brain function.

A study by The World Bank in 2006 also underscored sleep as a key factor in efficient learning, or the process of gaining optimal learning using few resources. The study reiterated the role of sleep in: (1) protecting and restoring memory, (2) advanced learning, and (3) enhancing mathematical ability and problem-solving. It further noted that "knowledge is better consolidated when people study at the time when they are supposed to be awake rather than, say, late-night sessions." It cited the need for research on "the memory capacity of the poor in low-income countries" to enable teachers to better help underprivileged students learn basic skills.

The effect of sleep on the human brain is just one of countless topics that have been examined by academics and specialists in various universities and medical institutions. A myriad of newer and even more specific research ideas likewise await the attention of avid scholars and inquisitive writers. Indeed, research is instrumental in building and improving knowledge and supporting existing knowledge with verifiable facts to facilitate learning.

2. It's a Means to Understand Issues and Increase Public Awareness

Using Research to Understand Current Issues

Television shows and movies—both fictional and nonfictional—ooze with research. For instance, Oprah Winfrey would have not achieved remarkable success as a news anchor and television show host had she eschewed doing her own research about certain topics and public figures. According to entrepreneur and lifestyle coach Paul C. Brunson, in his interview with emotional intelligence expert and author Justin Bariso (2017):

"Oprah spends a disproportionate amount of her time gathering information from communities of people outside of her core (different age groups, social classes, ethnicities, education levels, careers, etc.) and then she shares that information within her community."

This kind of effort shows the necessary role of research in helping others and raising social consciousness.

Using Research to Understand People

Many film and TV actors also take time to interview individuals to better understand their roles. Actors have worked with detectives, boxers, scientists, business owners, criminals, and teachers, among others to gain an inside understanding of what it's like to have a certain identity. Others even go through immersion so they can begin to understand their characters' issues better. This might look like living in jail or in a drug rehabilitation center for a while, gaining or losing a significant amount of weight, or learning to captain a sailboat. Many read literature, biographies, or journals to have a better view or context of the story they've been hired to tell.

In her 2017 article about Daniel Day-Lewis, Lynn Hirschberg described how the award-winning actor prepared for his role as dressmaker Reynolds Woodcock in Paul Thomas Anderson's film, *Phantom Thread*. She wrote:

"To become Woodcock, Day-Lewis, who is 60, watched archival footage of fashion shows from the 1940s and '50s, studied the lives of designers, and most important, learned to sew. He consulted with Cassie Davies-Strodder, then curator of fashion and textiles at the Victoria and Albert Museum, in London. And for many months he apprenticed under Marc Happel, who is head of the costume department at the New York City Ballet, watching intently and then helping to reconstruct the famous Marc Chagall costumes for a production of Firebird. At the end of the ballet season, Day-Lewis decided he needed to build a couture piece from scratch."

People both within and outside of the entertainment industry have, on occasion, belittled what actors do or even the profession of acting itself. However, professional thespians like Daniel Day-Lewis exert a great deal of effort to make their characters believable. The dedication they pour into studying their roles involves a tremendous amount of research.

Using Research to Create Realistic Fiction and Stories

A number of films, theater plays, broadcast dramas, and online videos present stories based on real-life events and problems. A serious writer or content producer sees how vital research is in substantiating the context of the stories they are telling to entertain and educate audiences through different media platforms.

As Terry Freedman opined in "The Importance of Research for ICT Teachers" (2011): "Research can shed light on issues we didn't even know existed, and can raise questions we hadn't realised even needed asking." Thus, almost all writers of both imaginary tales and non-fictive accounts do research, as doing so helps them create good stories and achieve credibility

3. It Helps Us Succeed in Business

The Importance of Research and Development (R&D)

Research benefits business. Many successful companies, such as those producing consumer goods or mass-market items, invest in research and development, or R and D. Different industries that involve science and engineering processes (like agriculture, food and beverage, manufacturing, healthcare and pharmaceuticals, computer software, semiconductor, information and communication technology, construction, robotics, aerospace, aviation, and energy) have high R and D expenses because it is critical to the creation and improvement of their products and services.

R and D can also help secure an advantage over competitors. Finding out how to make things happen more efficiently and differentiate a business's offerings from those of its competitors can raise a company's market value.

In addition, R and D is essential to supporting a country's economy. For instance, the United Kingdom's Department of Business Innovation and Skills, or BIS (now known as the Department for Business, Energy and Industrial Strategy), used to publish an annual R and D Scoreboard. The report served ". . . as a benchmarking tool for companies, investors and policymakers" for 20 years. However, due to the UK government's austerity measures, it has not been produced since 2010.

Market Research and Targeted Marketing

Research can also help a company maintain a positive commercial image, retain existing customers, and attract new customers through targeted marketing. Marketing is a type of communication, and for that communication to be effective, businesses need to understand their customers.

This usually happens through market research, which can involve examining psychological studies about consumption, hosting focus groups, beta testing products with a select group of customers, sending satisfaction surveys to existing customers, and researching the business's main competitors, among other strategies. The most successful businesses, large and small, base their product design, service offerings, and marketing communications on insights gleaned from thorough research processes.

4. It Allows Us to Disprove Lies and Support Truths

Background Research and Private Investigations

Have you ever experienced the feeling that your partner is having an affair behind your back? Some people would overlook this and say that it's better not to know; others though would take discreet action, hiring a private detective to find out for sure. What does research have to do with this situation? A lot. Doing research to reveal lies or truths involving personal affairs can contribute to either making a relationship work or breaking away from a dysfunctional one. For the monogamous lot, doing research to disprove or prove infidelity is one way to find out the truth.

Field Testing and Peer Reviews

Scientists also deal with research to test the validity and reliability of their claims or those of other scientists. Their integrity and competence depend on the quality of their research. Nevertheless, not everything scientists come up with gets accepted. Scientific work is typically peer-reviewed before being published. This means that when an individual publishes research, it is fact-checked and investigated for common biases, statistical errors, and methodological issues by others in the field before being shared with the scientific community at large.

Professional and credible journalists also undertake thorough research to establish the veracity of their stories. The 2003 movie *Shattered Glass* tells the rise-and-fall story of a real-life journalist who worked for *The New Republic* based in New York City. If fellow journalists hadn't debunked his stories as fabricated, Stephen Glass could have written even more dubious pieces that would have been taken at face value by readers of the publication.

Fact-Checking to Discover Research Bias, Propaganda, and Fake News

With the use of internet technology and social media, pseudo-journalism has become a social concern. Fake news took center stage during the 2016 presidential campaign period in the United States. For instance, Snopes.com, a rumor research site, debunked the following "news stories" posted online:

- An FBI agent believed to be responsible for the latest email leaks "pertinent to the investigation" into Hillary Clinton's private email server while she was Secretary of State, was found dead in an apparent murder-suicide. (Reported on November 5, 2016, by the *Denver Guardian*)

- In a final speech to the synod, Pope Francis endorsed Senator Bernie Sanders for President of the United States. (Reported on October 26, 2015, by the *National Report* and *USAToday.com.co)*

- Thousands of pre-marked ballots for Hillary Clinton and other Democratic candidates were found in a warehouse in Ohio. (Reported on September 30, 2016, by the *Christian Times Newspaper*)

- Assange: Bernie Sanders was threatened and told to drop out of the presidential race. (Reported on August 29, 2016, by *USA Supreme*)

- News outlets around the world are reporting on the news that Pope Francis has made the unprecedented decision to endorse US presidential candidate Donald Trump. (Reported in July 2016, by the *WTOE 5 News*)

- After gay club massacre, Phoenix LGBT officially endorses Trump. (Reported on June 13, 2016, by the *Gateway Pundit*)

- African-American supporter of Republican presidential candidate Donald Trump has died after allegedly sustaining gunshot wounds in the aftermath of Friday night's chaos in Chicago. (Reported on March 12, 2016, by the *Christian Times Newspaper*)

According to Pew Research, social media, especially Facebook, serves as a primary source of news for over 60 percent of adult Americans (Chang, Lefferman, Pedersen, and Martz, 2016). In addition to fueling social media company profits, fake news has become profitable for pseudo-journalists whose main goal is to attract reader clicks that lead to Google Adsense revenue.

Fact-checking to determine the truth is integral to the process of research. Murray, Social News, and UGC Hub (2016) suggest that before news readers share information on social media, they need to assess the integrity of the news source and check for similar news on legitimate media outlets.

Genuine journalists do not rely on imagination for their news reports, nor do they avoid doing research. They eschew propaganda and have no intention of misleading the public. They are messengers of useful information—not lies.

Opportunities for success come more easily when we're well informed.
Kelly Sikkema via Unsplash; Canva

5. It Is a Means to Find, Gauge, and Seize Opportunities

Research helps people nurture their potential and achieve goals by taking advantage of various opportunities. This can mean securing employment, being awarded scholarships or grants, securing project funding, initiating a business collaboration, finding budget travel opportunities, or securing other little wins.

Using Research to Maximize Job and Career Options

For those looking for a job or seeking greener pastures, research is necessary. With thorough research, an individual can increase their chances of finding employment by scouring job-posting sites, contacting employment agencies. Research can also help inform them if work opportunities are legitimate. Without research, the gullible-yet-hopeful jobseeker or traveling worker may fall prey to unscrupulous headhunters, bogus employment opportunities, or even full-on scams. Sites like Glassdoor and organizations like the Better Business Bureau allow job candidates to find out what experiences others have had with an employer they are considering or a placement agency they are thinking of using. After finding a free or low-cost academic course or skills-development training, students and professionals can assess their eligibility for certain roles and find out about application requirements and deadlines by conducting additional research.

Using Research to Maximize Investment

Research also benefits civil society and its members. Securing funding for projects and research initiatives is a top concern for those who want to address social issues. However, not all funding organizations accept proposals year-round, nor are they all interested in solving the same types of social problems. Thus, it is necessary to conduct research to find agencies whose missions match the objectives of particular advocacy programs or social-change projects.

An aspiring business owner can likewise meet potential investors through research. They can examine investor profiles to find a good fit in terms of vision, mission, goals work ethic, and available capital.

Some hobbies and interests are expensive to pursue. One of these is traveling. For budget-conscious tourists, searching for airfare and hotel promos, discount rides, and cheap markets is certainly a must to maximize the value of their money.

Seizing opportunities can broaden one's social network, raise one's awareness, or secure the support one direly needs to start a project or a business. Indeed, research contributes to a person's ability to make life-changing decisions. It encourages self-growth, participation in worthwhile causes, and productive living.

6. It Promotes a Love of Reading, Writing, Analyzing, and Sharing Valuable Information

Research for Critical Thinking

Research entails both reading and writing. These two literacy functions help maintain critical thinking and comprehension. Without these skills, research is far more difficult. Reading opens the mind to a vast reservoir of knowledge, while writing helps us express our own perspectives and transform our thoughts into more concrete ideas in a way others can understand.

Apart from reading and writing, listening and speaking are also integral to conducting research. Conducting interviews, attending knowledge-generating events, and participating in casual talks can help us gather information and formulate research topics. These things also facilitate our critical thinking process, much like reading and writing. Listening to experts discuss their work can help us analyze issues from new perspectives and add new techniques to our information-gathering arsenal.

Sharing Research for Wider Understanding

With the wide array of ideas floating around and the interconnectedness of people and places through the internet, scholars and non-scholars involved in research are able to share information with a larger audience. Some view this process as ego-boosting, while others see it as a means to stimulate interest and encourage further research into certain issues or situations.

Literacy is integral in improving a person's social and economic mobility and in increasing awareness, and research hones these basic life skills and makes learning a lifelong endeavor.

Exercising your mind is just as important as exercising your body.

7. It Provides Nourishment and Exercise for the Mind

Curiosity may kill the cat, but it also fuels the mind to seek answers. An article by Todd Johnson for College Admission Partners (n.d.) notes how scientific research in particular "helps students develop critical reasoning skills . . . helpful for any field of higher education . . ." The acts of searching for information and thinking critically serve as food for the brain, allowing our inherent creativity and logic to remain active. Keeping the mind active may also help prevent certain mental illnesses like Alzheimer's.

Critical Thinking and Mental Health

Several studies have shown that mentally stimulating activities like doing research can contribute to brain health. In "Educating the Brain to Avoid Dementia: Can Mental Exercise Prevent Alzheimer Disease?" Margaret Gatz (2005) enumerated research findings that support such a position. However, she also noted that there may be other factors involved in averting dementia and relates issues. One of these is intelligence. A study involving 11-year-old pupils in Scotland in 2000, for instance, pointed to intelligence quotient (IQ) scores as "predictive of future dementia risk". Gatz opined that clinical trials are needed and that "conclusions must be based on large samples, followed over a long period of time." She further posited:

". . . we have little evidence that mental practice will help prevent the development of dementia. We have better evidence that good brain health is multiply determined, that brain development early in life matters, and that genetic influences are of great importance in accounting for individual differences in cognitive reserve and in explaining who develops Alzheimer disease and who does not . . .

For older adults, health practices that could influence the brain include sound nutrition, sufficient sleep, stress management, treatment of mood or anxiety disorders, good vascular health, physical exercise, and avoidance of head trauma. But there is no convincing evidence that memory practice and other cognitively stimulating activities are sufficient to prevent Alzheimer disease; it is not just a case of "use it or lose it."

Gatz would have not formed such a perspective if she failed to conduct her own research about the effects of mentally stimulating activities on the human brain. This demonstrates how research can be both an exciting and challenging cerebral endeavor. Various studies may or may not support each other based on gathered information and other evidence. Data collection and analysis are vital aspects of the research process. These are mental activities that both expend mental energy and nurture the brain.

Indeed, doing research encourages people to explore possibilities, understand existing issues, and disprove fabrications. Without research, all of our technological advancements and other developments would have remained fantasies. Reading, writing, observing, and analyzing facilitate an inquisitive mind's quest for knowledge, learning, and wisdom. Research is a bridge that we must cross to achieve all of our goals—both personal and societal.

Research Basics for High School Students by Journal Storage (JSTOR)

How to Conduct Research for Beginners

Research is about contributing to a growing pool of knowledge and information. Although we are inherently curious as kids and young adults and often conduct informal research without even realizing it, there is a methodology for conducting formal, academic research. Use the following tips to get you started:

1. Organize and Prioritize Your Available Resources

It is important to set out a suitable timeframe for your project and to assemble all the necessary literature, find sources of information, and establish a financial budget (if applicable).

2. Identify the Central Question That Will Be Explored in Your Paper

Generally, there is only one research question per project, so if your project prompts you to engage with several different questions, it could be a good idea to break it up into several papers. For example, you may write a paper on both the impact and the validity of a written consent agreement form at a medical facility. Strong research questions are specific, original, and relevant to society and the scientific community.

3. Research Existing Literature Related to Your Topic on the Appropriate Database

Scientific journals are a good place to start. Identify the contribution that each study provides in the context of your research question. Examine relationships and methods of data interpretation with a critical mindset.

How to Find Peer-Reviewed Research in Academic Journals

THE ELEMENTS OF A RESEARCH PAPER

Research papers are far less daunting when you break them down into their individual components.

Element	Purpose
Abstract	Summarize your purpose and design. Try to use fewer than 300 words.
Introduction	State the problem and review the relevant literature.
Methods	Discuss your study design, including any instruments you will be using, and outline the strategy you will use to analyze the data.

Research papers are far less daunting when you break them down into their individual components.

Element	Purpose
Results	Restate your research question and describe your findings.
Discussion	Discuss your findings in the context of your overall question as well as previous literature and research. Make suggestions for future research projects on the subject.
Conclusion	Restate your thesis and summarize your main points.

3

COMMON ERRORS IN THE RESEARCH PROCESS

Designing a research project and writing a paper is no simple feat. Participants should be ready to dedicate an ample amount of time to avoid burnout. Here are some common mistakes that are made in both the setup of the project and the research paper itself.

Population Mistakes

Population mistakes are as avoidable as they are common in research. It helps to define the characteristics of the group that you wish to sample from in your project so you can specify the population in question. For instance, if you are asking a question about the attitudes of michigan residents, it would be important to make sure the population you're sampling from includes all counties in Michigan so your data isn't skewed to favor people from a specific and relatively homogenous area.

Sampling Mistakes

Sampling mistakes are another common research issue.. Be sure to broaden the sample if you feel as though it is too small toe generalize. For example, if 10% of therapists at Happy Clinic are dependent on marijuana, this does not mean that 10% of therapists in the nation are as well.

Sample-Selection Process Errors

The sample-selection process is another potential research issue. If you were randomly choosing participants in person, let's say at the mall, you would not want to only seek participants who are receptive and agreeable. These are usually your friends and acquaintances whose characteristics are similar to yours. Replace your non-probability selection method with true random samples from a defined population. These are usually the most scientifically sound.

Common Problems With Research Papers

- The research question or aim is vague or is not specific enough.
- The structure of the paper is unorganized.
- The introduction is an extensive list of previous findings and doesn't propose anything new.
- Tables do not relate to the main question.
- The method and results sections are not defined in detail.
- The discussion does not answer the stated research question.

HOW TO IMPROVE YOUR RESEARCH SKILLS

Are you interested in further developing your ability to do research? The following suggestions can help you hone your craft as a researcher while learning new things all the while.

- Read books and articles about research. If you do not have a computer with an internet connection, you can go to the library, a nearby bookstore, or ask a close friend or relative to lend you their smartphone or laptop so you can look for books or articles about research. If you have access to the internet, you can watch online tutorial videos on research.

- Watch films and read different kinds of books, including fiction and nonfiction. These sources can ignite your curiosity and drive you to seek more information. You might want to jot down notes about the topics that were discussed and/or what you learned. You might wonder why this is part of the research process. Watching movies, reading books, and writing notes helps hone your comprehension and ability to analyze. These can improve your vocabulary and help you in finding your voice as a researcher.

- Attend training seminars, workshops, and conferences aimed at deepening your knowledge and honing your critical-thinking skills. These events are conducted by various organizations, particularly universities and "think tank" agencies. Use search engines to look for these opportunities, as well as for scholarships that could help you finance your participation in these activities.

- Search for reputable researchers in your field of interest, especially if you plan to pursue collegiate or postgraduate studies. You could email an academic, a scientist, or another professional to inquire about their opinion on your thesis or dissertation topic. Having a research mentor can help you gain a broader understanding of what research is all about. They can likewise enrich your experience and insights as a researcher.

Go Forth and Research!

The human quest to seek knowledge, satisfy one's sense of wonder, develop more abilities, connect with others, and understand society is integral to research. Perpetuating truths (and debunking lies and myths) requires inquisitive minds and priceless integrity. As the world continues to evolve, doing research becomes more important and remains a skill with enduring rewards.

This content is accurate and true to the best of the author's knowledge and is not meant to substitute for formal and individualized advice from a qualified professiona

4

QUESTIONS & ANSWERS

Question: To invest in research is to invest in a better future. Does this statement sound true? If so, justify your answer.

Answer: It is true. If you have read my hub, you would be able to discern why. It is important that you think of the answer yourself, as it will help you improve your analytical skills.

Question: What are the purposes of research?

Answer: My hub somehow answers your question. The purpose also depends on your objectives or target goals for pursuing a certain research topic.

Question: How does research contribute to quality education?

Answer: My article is not about quality education, but it talks about the importance of research in general, including its role in generating knowledge and in facilitating effective learning. Please read my article, if you have time. Doing so might be able to help you gain some insights and think of the answer to your question. You might want to ponder on your definition of "quality education" and look for studies and other references discussing it.

Question: What is the role of research in society?

Answer: Research is critical to societal development. It generates knowledge, provides useful information, and helps decision-making, among others.

Question: What is the concept of research?

Answer: The concept of research depends on your objectives for doing it. Research is essentially an intellectual process that helps you examine a certain phenomenon or topic based on personal, academic, and/or corporate interests. There are different methodologies and tools for doing it. Please conduct further research to help you answer your question.

Question: What is the role of research in development?

Answer: Research is critical in various development endeavors. Economic development requires determining what factors affect market forces and business environment, including laws that may either block or boost investments. Organizational development likewise entails identifying what policies are either beneficial or detrimental to achieving institutional goals. Personal development also involves finding useful public and private resources that may help an individual improve his/her skills and knowledge. Attaining development is challenging, and doing research allows stakeholders to gain necessary information and insights as they pursue set targets.

Thanks for the question. If you need an answer with citation, I highly encourage you to do your own research and develop your skills and knowledge as a researcher.

Question: What are the main objectives of doing research?

Answer: My hub provides several reasons as to why doing research is essential in general, including (1) to build knowledge and facilitate efficient learning, (2) to understand various issues, (3) to know the truth and prove lies, and (4) to seek opportunities, among others. It somehow answers your question. However, if you are referring to a certain topic, then it does not provide the primary objectives based on the topic of your research. In this case, the main objectives largely depend on the reasons why you would like to do that particular research.

Question: Can you give offer some examples that describe number six?

Answer: 6. A Seed to Love Reading, Writing, Analyzing, and Sharing Valuable Information

When your teacher asks you to research a topic that you want, think of topics that you find interesting. If you are into anime, for instance, take steps to know more about anime. Knowing about anime goes beyond merely watching it. If you read about anime, write about what you read, analyze the nature of anime, and then share your findings. That's only one order of actions taken by a researcher.

There are people who initially write what they know about a certain topic like space exploration, while others analyze a situation or an issue first before reading and writing about it. Some researchers use previous studies as a take-off point in doing further research about a topic, primarily to determine if their study or experiment will reach or replicate the same findings or conclusions.

I hope what I said has somehow answered your query. Otherwise, you might want to research further the connection between researching reading, writing, analyzing, and sharing one's knowledge with other people.

Question: Which is the best topic for research?

Answer: It really depends on your interests and if you are doing it as a student or as an independent researcher. Otherwise, you should talk to a teacher or superior to help you figure out what research topic you would like to explore.

Question: What is the importance of identifying a problem in doing research?

Answer: Some people do research out of curiosity, while others do it because it is part of their job. Identifying a problem provides a basis for doing research. It also helps in figuring out the objectives and limitations of the research. These are just what I can think of at the moment. If you want an answer with citation, I encourage you to do further research related to your question.

Question: What are the subheadings of a research report?

Answer: My hub is about why doing research is important. It is not about how to write a research report and its different parts. This could be a good topic for a future hub though, so thank you for asking.

Please consider looking for information related to research report writing that is posted on university-based websites. These are both useful and authoritative sources of such information. However, research report format, including main headings and subheadings, varies from one organization to another. You may choose which among the available options you would like to adopt in your research report.

Question: When should research be undertaken?

Answer: My article somehow answers your question. A person may undertake research when he or she is curious about or seeking the latest info about a certain topic, or has to submit a paper. It is also conducted when one's job requires it or to verify certain information. There are other moments when it is undertaken. I suggest that you do your own research about it.

Question: What are the characteristics of research?

Answer: A few characteristics of research would include (1) objectivity, (2) accuracy of information, (3) understandable discussion of related literature, collected data, and analysis of results, and (4) written by credible and ethical experts/authors, among others.

Question: Why is it important to conduct historical research?

Answer: Historical research helps verify certain facts and information about a topic. There are others reasons why it is undertaken. I suggest that you use academic websites to help you answer your question.

Question: What are the objects that are important in research?

Answer: Some of the things that are important in doing research are writing materials (paper/notebook and pen), reading materials (books, articles, journals, etc.), and communication devices (mobile phone, landline phone). Having a laptop or desktop computer or a smartphone that has access to the Internet and printing machine can certainly help you:

(1) write research ideas and drafts,

(2) read online references related to your research topic,

(3) facilitate printing of your reading materials and research manuscripts, and

(4) communicate with your research respondents, interviewees, mentors, and other resource persons via email, chat, and/or video conference.

It is also helpful to have a school library card or resident identification card that you can use to access books and other materials in a nearby community library. If your research involves interviewing people, then a tape recorder or digital recorder would be useful.

I may have missed several other objects, so please do further research to help you answer your question.

Question: What should I do in order to write a good research proposal?

Answer: Though my hub does not talk about how to write a research proposal (and a good one at that), I suggest that you ask yourself what topics would you like to examine further. For instance, if the field is broad like health, then list down health-related topics that you find interesting. Choose 1-3 issues that you would like to explore. Why more than one? Just for contingency in case, the others seem harder to do, if not impossible. The format, criteria, and requirements will depend on your teacher, the funding agency, and your preferred academic program/department at your chosen college or university.

Based on experience, a research proposal is considered "good" if it offers clear purpose/objectives, methods, potential benefits to stakeholders, and budget (if applicable). Some organizations ask for monitoring, evaluation, and sustainability plans. There are also agencies and assessors who are meticulous when it comes to the use of the English language, particularly grammar and spelling. Thus, you might want to hire a professional editor and a proofreader to help you polish your research proposal. Otherwise, there are online materials that you can use to help you improve your English writing skills.

5

10 REASONS WHY RESEARCH IS IMPORTANT

No matter what career field you're in or how high up you are, there's always more to learn. The same applies to your personal life. No matter how many experiences you have or how diverse your social circle, there are things you don't know. Research unlocks the unknowns, lets you explore the world from different perspectives, and fuels a deeper understanding. In some areas, research is an essential part of success. In others, it may not be absolutely necessary, but it has many benefits. Here are ten reasons why research is important:

1. Research expands your knowledge base

The most obvious reason to do research is that you'll learn more. There's always more to learn about a topic, even if you are already well-versed in it. If you aren't, research allows you to build on any personal experience you have with the subject. The process of research opens up new opportunities for learning and growth.

2. Research gives you the latest information

Research encourages you to find the most recent information available. In certain fields, especially scientific ones, there's always new information and discoveries being made. Staying updated prevents you from falling behind and giving info that's inaccurate or doesn't paint the whole picture. With the latest info, you'll be better equipped to talk about a subject and build on ideas.

3. Research helps you know what you're up against

In business, you'll have competition. Researching your competitors and what they're up to helps you formulate your plans and strategies. You can figure out what sets you apart. In other types of research, like medicine, your research might identify diseases, classify symptoms, and come up with ways to tackle them. Even if your "enemy" isn't an actual person or competitor, there's always some kind of antagonist force or problem that research can help you deal with.

4. Research builds your credibility

People will take what you have to say more seriously when they can tell you're informed. Doing research gives you a solid foundation on which you can build your ideas and opinions. You can speak with confidence about what you know is accurate. When you've done the research, it's much harder for someone to poke holes in what you're saying. Your research should be focused on the best sources. If your "research" consists of opinions from non-experts, you won't be very credible. When your research is good, though, people are more likely to pay attention.

5. Research helps you narrow your scope

When you're circling a topic for the first time, you might not be exactly sure where to start. Most of the time, the amount of work ahead of you is overwhelming. Whether you're writing a paper or formulating a business plan, it's important to narrow the scope at some point. Research helps you identify the most unique and/or important themes. You can choose the themes that fit best with the project and its goals.

6. Research teaches you better discernment

Doing a lot of research helps you sift through low-quality and high-quality information. The more research you do on a topic, the better you'll get at discerning what's accurate and what's not. You'll also get better at discerning the gray areas where information may be technically correct but used to draw questionable conclusions.

7. Research introduces you to new ideas

You may already have opinions and ideas about a topic when you start researching. The more you research, the more viewpoints you'll come across. This encourages you to entertain new ideas and perhaps take a closer look at yours. You might change your mind about something or, at least, figure out how to position your ideas as the best ones.

8. Research helps with problem-solving

Whether it's a personal or professional problem, it helps to look outside yourself for help. Depending on what the issue is, your research can focus on what others have done before. You might just need more information, so you can make an informed plan of attack and an informed decision. When you know you've collected good information, you'll feel much more confident in your solution.

9. Research helps you reach people

Research is used to help raise awareness of issues like climate change, racial discrimination, gender inequality, and more. Without hard facts, it's very difficult to prove that climate change is getting worse or that gender inequality isn't progressing as quickly as it should. The public needs to know what the facts are, so they have a clear idea of what "getting worse" or "not progressing" actually means. Research also entails going beyond the raw data and sharing real-life stories that have a more personal impact on people.

10. Research encourages curiosity

Having curiosity and a love of learning take you far in life. Research opens you up to different opinions and new ideas. It also builds discerning and analytical skills. The research process rewards curiosity. When you're committed to learning, you're always in a place of growth. Curiosity is also good for your health. Studies show curiosity is associated with higher levels of positivity, better satisfaction with life, and lower anxiety.

BENEFITS OF CONDUCTING RESEARCH

The benefits of conducting research include increasing personal knowledge and contributing to humanity, as well as developing skills and interests.

Market Research There are several different types of research and benefits to each. Market research enables companies to explore new and appropriate strategies for advertising and distributing their products or services. It also allows them to identify possible causes of poor sales, such as falling brand awareness among the public or competition from other brands.

Nonprofit Research Research for a nonprofit organization or for the greater good allows people to better understand the ever-changing needs of the community. This not only helps validate a case when it comes time to ask for funding, but also allows for better training of professionals so that they are able to aid the community. Research allows new programs to be implemented with the hope of achieving community success.

Medical and Scientific Research Perhaps the field that benefits most by research is the medical and scientific field. Proper research helps pave the way for vaccines and preventative medicine, which can alleviate disease before it occurs. Research also aids in finding cures for disease. It allows medication to be thoroughly tested and evaluated. Scientific research covers a broader spectrum, allowing for psychological testing and solutions in the mental health field, with double-blind and other types of research experiments.

Combination Often, many types of different research are combined. For example, a new prescription drug may be heavily tested and evaluated, and found to help those who suffer from clinical depression. Perhaps it is approved by the FDA, but more research is needed. Next, a double-blind, controlled psychological study is performed on subjects who suffer from depression. If these results are found to be satisfactory, then pharmaceutical companies have to perform the correct market research to decide how to advertise to patients who may benefit from the drug. There may also be a correlating study on how depression affects the community as a whole. All of these branches of research come together to try to control or solve a problem.

Further Benefits There are some further generic benefits that apply to all types of research. Research improves overall quality. For a nonprofit, it can improve quality of life in the community. For medical research, it can improve the quality of a drug or medical procedure. Research also puts knowledge in the hands of everyday citizens. Most research findings and studies are available to the general public so that they do not have to do the research themselves. This research expands knowledge and practices in many different types of fields, allows students to get interested in topics and allows organizations to ask for funding where it is needed. Having access to scientific literature can help everyone, from the doctor to the everyday average Joe.

One final benefit of research is that it also facilitates statistical analysis. Quantitative scientific findings, for instance, tend to be represented numerically, and can therefore be easily assessed for significance and implications.

KINDS OF RESEARCH

According to MCcOMBES (2020), When you start planning a research project, developing research questions and creating a research design, you will have to make various decisions about the type of research you want to do.

There are many ways to categorize different types of research. The words you use to describe your research depend on your discipline and field. In general, though, the form your research design takes will be shaped by:

- The type of knowledge you aim to produce
- The type of data you will collect and analyze
- The sampling methods, timescale and location of the research

This article takes a look at some common distinctions made between different types of research and outlines the key differences between them.

TYPES OF RESEARCH AIMS

Type of research	**What's the difference?**	**What to consider**
Basic vs applied	Basic research aims to **develop knowledge, theories and predictions**, while applied research aims to **develop techniques, products and procedures**.	Do you want to expand scientific understanding or solve a practical problem?
Exploratory vs explanatory	Exploratory research aims to **explore the main aspects of an under-researched problem**, while explanatory research aims to **explain the causes and consequences of a well-defined problem**.	How much is already known about your research problem? Are you conducting initial research on a newly-identified issue, or seeking precise conclusions about an established issue?

| Inductive vs deductive | Inductive research aims to **develop a theory**, while deductive research aims to **test a theory**. | Is there already some theory on your research problem that you can use to develop hypotheses, or do you want to propose new theories based on your findings? |

Types of research aims

The first thing to consider is what kind of knowledge your research aims to contribute.

Types of research data

The next thing to consider is what type of data you will collect. Each kind of data is associated with a range of specific research methods and procedures.

TYPES OF RESEARCH DATA

Type of research	What's the difference?	What to consider
Primary vs secondary	Primary data is **collected directly by the researcher** (e.g. through interviews or experiments), while secondary data **has already been collected by someone else** (e.g. in government surveys or scientific publications).	How much data is already available on your topic? Do you want to collect original data or analyze existing data (e.g. through a literature review)?
Qualitative vs quantitative	Qualitative research methods **focus on words and meanings**, while quantitative research methods **focus on numbers and statistics**.	Is your research more concerned with measuring something or interpreting something? You can also create a mixed methods

Descriptive vs experimental	Descriptive research gathers data **without controlling any variables**, while experimental research **manipulates and controls variables to determine cause and effect**.	research design that has elements of both. Do you want to identify characteristics, patterns and correlations or test causal relationships between variables?

Types of sampling, timescale and location

Finally, you have to consider three closely related questions: how will you select the subjects or participants of the research? When and how often will you collect data from your subjects? And where will the research take place?

Types of research subjects, timescales and locations

Type of research	What's the difference?	What to consider
Probability vs non-probability sampling	Probability sampling allows you to **generalize your findings to a broader population**, while non-probability sampling allows you to draw conclusions **only about the specific subjects of the research**.	Do you want to produce generalizable knowledge that applies to many contexts or detailed knowledge about a specific context (e.g. in a case study)?
Cross-sectional vs longitudinal	Cross-sectional studies **gather data at a single point in**	Is your research question focused on understanding the current

	time, while longitudinal studies **gath er data at several points in time**.	situation or tracking changes over time?
Field vs laboratory	Field research takes place in **a natural or real-world setting**, while laboratory research takes place in **a controlled and constructe d setting**.	Do you want to find out how something occurs in the real world or draw firm conclusions about cause and effect? Laboratory experiments have higher intern al validity but lower extern al validity.
Fixed vs flexible	In a fixed research design the subjects, timescale and location are **set**	Do you want to test hypotheses and establish generalizable facts, or explore

before data collection begins, while in a flexible design these aspects may **develop through the data collection process**.

concepts and develop understanding? For measuring, testing and making generalizations, a fixed research design has higher validity and reliability.

Choosing between all these different research types is part of the process of creating your research design, which determines exactly how the research will be conducted. But the type of research is only the first step: next, you have to make more concrete decisions about your research methods and the details of the study.

6

MORE ON THE TYPES OF RESEARCH

This article is from Susan White in 2019.

Research and science especially go hand in hand. When we talk about science, the other word which comes in our mind is research. Research helps in scientific discoveries. Every new medicine is a product of long research. But the word research is now not limited to the field of science only. In almost every discipline different types of research are present currently. Research is a vital part of the development and discoveries of new things in all academic subjects. From science to psychology every subject now has some and some kind of research work in it.

Okay let us review....

So today with the help of this blog I am going to talk about:

- What Research is?
- Two main types of research
- Difference types of research and a thin line of demarcation in them
- What research is not?
- Why is research helpful to students?

WHAT IS RESEARCH AGAIN?

Research is a systematic inquiry on a specific topic. When you want to get the information on a particular topic, you take a process to enhance your knowledge. There are different types of research out there. But it depends on you what type you prefer.

A lot of casual researches these days begins with a Google query ("Who, what, how?") and you will end on a Wiki page. Getting informative data is comparatively easy. The knowledge already exists. You just have to search a trustworthy source for it. Assessing credibility is the hard part.

Why is research helpful to students?

This question may come to your psyche while you are in your academic career. You often think that what is a need of doing a research work? Why universities want us to carry out research. Then read below to find your answer.

Answer of the question raised above

- It teaches them to inquire about things that are said and done, rather than accepting or rejecting them at face value;
- It teaches them to gather evidence for things that are said and done, before making decisions;
- Research teaches them how to gather that evidence, in ways that minimize bias;
- It teaches them to consider alternatives before making decisions;
- in the process, they learn to evaluate things that are said and done from the weaknesses and strengths of those arguments or events;
- therefore it increases the chances that their decisions are going to be helpful/realistic ones;
- It increases the chances that any advice that the student gives will be well-judged;

- It demonstrates that the experience of doing real-world research is different from the idea of how that research will go into the researcher's imagination, and this insight is valuable. Humans are very prone to constructing ideas from nothing other than what is in their heads, and being able to compare that to reality is important for living a coping life.

TWO MAIN TYPES OF RESEARCH

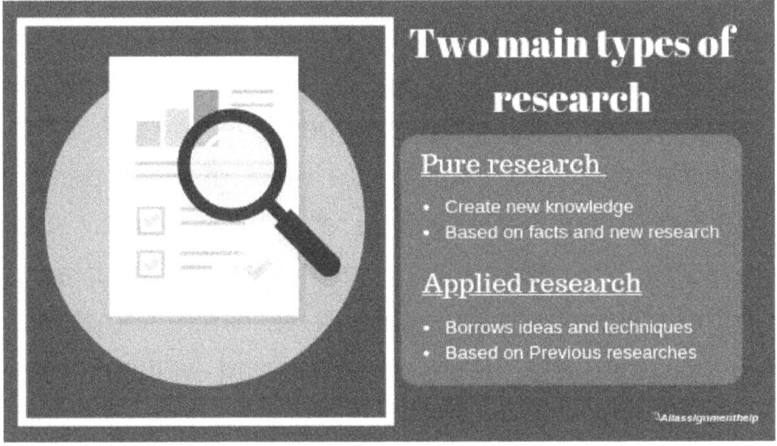

Pure research is carried out to generate new human knowledge. To uncover new facts or fundamental principles you need pure research. The researcher wants to advance in a specific field, for example, neuroscience, by answering a specific question, such as "Why do humans sleep?" Pure research is based on experimentation and observation. The results of your research are published in peer-reviewed journals. This is *science.* Rigorous standards and methodologies exist to preserve objectivity and ensure the credibility of conclusions. (Things get squishy when corporations fund ostensibly pure research, as they frequently do.)

Applied research borrows ideas and techniques from pure research to serve a specific real-world goal. Goals are like creating a super soldier or improving the quality of hospital care or finding new ways to market any product. While ethics are as important, and methods can be more relaxed. By this, I meant changing the questions you ask while doing a study, or making the most of an imperfect sample group because you're tight on time. Your research is successful only to the extent that it adds to the stated goal. As with pure research, sometimes you accidentally discover something valuable you weren't even looking for, and that's a fantastic bonus.

Different types of research and a thin line of demarcation in them

So now you have understood about two main types of research in the above paragraph. But that is not enough. There are further types of research presentations. You may say these are the subdivision of above-mentioned types. Now you will learn about different types of research and basic difference in them.

DIFFERENCE BETWEEN VARIOUS RESEARCH TYPES

DESCRIPTIVE VS. ANALYTICAL

In a Descriptive research you do before you know what you're doing. This research leads to ideas and helps in defining the problem.

Analytical research never gives you the final answers to your research questions. But it explores the research topic on different levels.

APPLIED VS. FUNDAMENTAL

Applied research works by finding a solution for an immediate problem. These problems are faced by society or by industry.

Fundamental research is concerned with the formulation of a theory. It is an add-on to the already existing scientific knowledge.

QUALITATIVE VS. QUANTITATIVE

Quantitative research is the measurement of quantity. It is applicable to the things which can be measured in terms of quantity.

Qualitative research is based on quality. Something related to quality or kind. For example, when we investigate the human behavior.

CONCEPTUAL VS. EMPIRICAL

Conceptual research is that related to some abstract idea(s) or theory. It is generally used by philosophers and thinkers to develop new concepts.

Empirical research relies an experience or observation alone, often without due regard for system and theory. It is data based research, coming up with conclusions.

Generative vs. exploratory research

This is the research you do before you know what you're doing. This research leads to ideas and helps in defining the problem. Don't think of this as just the earliest research. Even if you're working on a current product or service, you might be looking for ideas. You need ideas for additional features. Generative research includes interviews, reviewing existing literature, and field observation,

Exploratory research, as the name says, intends to explore the research questions. It does not make to give conclusive or final solutions for the existing problems. Exploratory research is conducted with an aim to study a problem that does not have any solution yet.

The research is done in order to understand the nature of the problem. It is not done to provide conclusive evidence. But it helps in the better understanding of the problem. When a researcher conducts exploratory research, he/she should be willing to change his/her direction when new data reveals.

Exploratory research never gives you the final or conclusive answers to your research questions. But it explores the research topic on different levels. It has been seen that exploratory research is an initial stage of research. Exploratory research provides a basis of conclusive research. It will help in making of research design, sampling methodology and data collection method. Exploratory research tackles new problems on which no research has been done.

Descriptive vs. Analytical

Descriptive research consists of surveys and fact-finding inquiries of various kinds. The major reason to carry out descriptive research is describing the state of affairs as it exists at present. When we do descriptive result in social science and business research, we use the term Ex post facto research for descriptive research work. The main feature of this method is that the researcher doesn't have control over the variables; he can only report things like what has happened or what is happening.

Most of the ex post facto research projects are made for descriptive studies. In these studies, the researcher seeks to measure items. Examples are; frequency of shopping, preferences of people, or similar data. Ex post facto studies also count attempts by researchers to discover causes, even when controlling variables is out of their hands. The methods of research use for descriptive research are survey methods of every kind. It includes comparative and co-relational methods. Whereas, in analytical research, Research use facts or already available information. He critically evaluates and analyzes the material.

Applied vs. Fundamental

Research can be of two types. One is applied (or action) research. Second is fundamental (to basic or pure) research. Applied research works by finding a solution for an immediate problem. These problems are faced by society or by industry whereas fundamental research is primarily concerned with the formulation of a theory. "Gathering knowledge for knowledge's sake is termed 'pure' or 'basic' research." Research which is more concerned with a natural phenomenon or relating to pure mathematics is fundamental research. Those research studies which are based on human behavior are also examples of fundamental research.

But applied research is based at conclusions. These conclusions are facing a concrete social or business problem. Applied research is to identify social, economic or political trends. These trends may affect a particular institution or copy research or marketing research. Thus, the basic aim of applied research is to find a solution to practical problems. Fundamental research is for finding information that has a broad base of applications. It is an add-on to the already existing scientific knowledge.

Quantitative vs. Qualitative

Quantitative research is recognized by its name. It is the measurement of quantity or amount. It is applicable to all things which we can measure in terms of quantity. Qualitative research is simply means quality. Something related to or involving quality or kind is qualitative research. For example, when we investigate the reason behind human behavior. This type of research is to discover underlying motives and desires, using in-depth interviews for the purpose. Other techniques of such research are sentence completion tests, word association tests, story completion tests.

Attitude or opinion research is also an example of kinds of qualitative research. Other examples are how people feel about a particular institution. Behavioral science has an important place for qualitative research. The aim of this research type is to discover the motives of human behavior. Through these researches, we can analyze the factors affecting behavior. This will further help in to motivate people to behave in a proper manner.

Conceptual research vs. Empirical research

Conceptual research is related to some abstract ideas or theory. It is mostly used by thinkers and philosophers to develop new concepts or to reinterpret existing ones. On the other hand, empirical research relies on experience or observation alone, often without due regard for system and theory. It is data-based research, coming up with conclusions which are capable of being verified by observation or experiment.

We can also call it as an experimental type of research; in such research, it is necessary to get the facts first, at their source, and actively to go about doing certain things to stimulate the production of desired information. In such research, the researcher must first provide himself with a working hypothesis or guess as to the probable results. He then works to get enough facts (data) to prove or disprove his hypothesis. He then sets up experimental designs which he thinks will manipulate the persons or the materials concerned so as to bring forth the desired information.

Such research is thus characterized by the experimenter's control over the variables under study and his deliberate manipulation of one of them to study its effects. Empirical research is appropriate when the proof is sought that certain variables affect other variables in some way. Evidence that is gathered through empirical studies or experiments, is today considered to be the most powerful support possible for a given hypothesis.

When a student begins his research work, he often does not pay attention to different types of research. In my opinion, selecting a particular research type from types mentioned above of research is of vital importance. You cannot neglect your research work and get away with it. If you find difficulty in doing research, you can get in touch with our Australian assignment experts for academic writing.

What research is not?

WHAT RESEARCH IS NOT?

Research work is not about asking people what they like and what not

When you begin interviewing people involved in business decisions, you will hear them saying what they like and don't like. "Like" word doesn't suits a critical thinker. On subconscious level, we all wish that things we do to be liked. So it's easy to treat likability as a leading success indicator. But the concept of "liking" is as subjective as it is empty. Getting a like is a superficial mental state unmoored from any specific behavior. This means you can't get any useful insights from any given individual reporting that they like or hate a particular thing.

Research is not a political tool

Don't let your methods come out of a fake desire. By this, I meant to show yourself a smart or conform with other person's picture of research. Often clients will argue for doing interviews in a usability lab even when it isn't appropriate, just because it feels research. You'll need to explain and brief them why interviews with method and purpose are more valuable and correct than having a social conversation with a random person.

In the best possibilities, you can bring up the real-world facts and insights you collect to bring an other's perspective to internal debates and power struggles that threaten your ability to get good work done. At the very least, it's up to everyone participating in the research to hold the line and not let interpersonal dynamics influence your findings. Watch out for those who would use information gathering for political purposes or as a popularity contest.

It is not a defense of opinions

Research is also not a defense of opinions. The aim of research work is to reveal and bring out the facts and truth on papers. You have to avoid a different situation with the opposite party's opinions (unless you need to write a persuasive research paper).

Conclusion

So I hope after reading the above information, you may get a good hand over types of research. Let's have quick recall of the things we have discussed in the blog. Firstly I have discussed the purpose of research for students. What importance does a research work held in a students life? After that, I have explained you the two basic types of research, i.e., applied research and pure research. Moving on further I have explained you the further types of research with a small comparison. In the end, I discussed what research is not. I hope this blog fulfilled the purpose and looking for your feedback.

Kindly provide your feedback and help me to improve. Thank you for reading.

Insight us

Allassignmenthelp.com is a perfect destination for all the students looking out for **assignment help online**. We have a pool of academic expert writers who have expertise in various subjects. They have skills and expertise in writing essays, research articles, dissertation, and various academic tasks. Visit our website and take the benefits such as:

- Plagiarism free work
- Discounts and cash back on assignments
- On time delivery
- And many more

WHAT ARE THE DIFFERENT TYPES OF RESEARCH AGAIN?

According to Melanson (2020), there are many ways to categorize the different types of research. For example, research in different fields can be called different types of research, such as scientific research, social research, medical research, environmental research and so forth. The research methods that are used and purposes of the research also can be used to categorize the different types of research. A few of these types of research include quantitative and qualitative research; observational and experimental research; and basic, applied and developmental research.

Again....

Quantitative and Qualitative

Observational research can take place in the field, or in natural settings.

Quantitative research is the collecting of objective numerical data. Features are classified and counted, and statistical models are constructed to analyze and explain the information that has been gathered. Some of the tools used for this type of research include questionnaires that are given to test subjects, equipment that is used to measure something and databases of existing information. The goal of quantitative research is to compile statistical evidence, so the questionnaires used in this method typically include yes-or-no questions or multiple-choice questions rather than open-ended questions such as essay questions.

Qualitative data is typically gathered through interviews.

Unlike quantitative research, qualitative research is subjective and seeks to describe or interpret whatever is being researched. Instead of numbers, this type of research provides information in the form of words or visual representations. It relies on the researcher to observe, record what happens, such as participants' answers to open-ended questions, subjects' behavior or the results of experiments. Case studies are common examples of qualitative research.

Observational and Experimental

Medical research may take place in a lab.

Observational research is the collection of information without interference or input from the researcher. It is the examination of things as they naturally or inherently are. The researcher simply observes, measures or records what occurs. That information is then analyzed and used to draw conclusions.

This is in contrast with experimental research, in which the researcher sets the parameters or conditions and is able to change them to determine their effects. Experimental research often occurs in laboratories but can occur anywhere. It merely requires the researcher to be able to control one or more conditions of the experiment. This method helps researchers understand how certain variables — the different aspects or conditions that can change — can affect whatever it is they are studying.

Basic, Applied and Developmental

Social research examines how societal conditions such as poverty affect people.

When the purpose of research is simply to reveal or discover what is true, it can be called basic research. This type of research involves exploring that which is not known or understood. Applied research is taking what is already known and looking for ways to use it, such as to solve problems. Developmental research is similar to applied research but focuses on using what is already known to improve products or existing technology or to create something new.

7

A DEEPER LOOK ON QUANTITATIVE RESEARCH

According to Bhandari (2021), Quantitative research is the process of collecting and analyzing numerical data. It can be used to find patterns and averages, make predictions, test causal relationships, and generalize results to wider populations.

Quantitative research is the opposite of qualitative research, which involves collecting and analyzing non-numerical data (e.g. text, video, or audio).

Quantitative research is widely used in the natural and social sciences: biology, chemistry, psychology, economics, sociology, marketing, etc.

Quantitative research question examples

- What is the demographic makeup of Singapore in 2020?
- How has the average temperature changed globally over the last century?
- Does environmental pollution affect the prevalence of honey bees?
- Does working from home increase productivity for people with long commutes?

Quantitative research methods

You can use quantitative research methods for descriptive, correlational or experimental research.

- In descriptive research, you simply seek an overall summary of your study variables.

QUANTITATIVE RESEARCH METHODS

Research method	How to use	Example
Experiment	Control or manipulate an independent variable to measure its effect on a dependent variable.	To test whether an intervention can reduce procrastination in college students, you give equal-sized groups either a procrastination intervention or a comparable task. You compare self-ratings of procrastination behaviors between the groups after the intervention.
Survey	Ask questions of a group of people in-person, over-the-phone or online.	You distribute questionnaires with rating scales to first-year international college students to investigate their experiences of culture shock.
(Systematic)	Identify a	To study college

observation	behavior or occurrence of interest and monitor it in its natural setting.	classroom participation, you sit in on classes to observe them, counting and recording the prevalence of active and passive behaviors by students from different backgrounds.
Secondary research	Collect data that has been gathered for other purposes e.g., national surveys or historical records.	To assess whether attitudes towards climate change have changed since the 1980s, you collect relevant questionnaire data from widely available longitudinal studies.

- In correlational research, you investigate relationships between your study variables.
- In experimental research, you systematically examine whether there is a cause-and-effect relationship between variables.

Correlational and experimental research can both be used to formally test hypotheses, or predictions, using statistics. The results may be generalized to broader populations based on the sampling method used.

To collect quantitative data, you will often need to use operational definitions that translate abstract concepts (e.g., mood) into observable and quantifiable measures (e.g., self-ratings of feelings and energy levels).

Quantitative data analysis

Once data is collected, you may need to process it before it can be analyzed. For example, survey and test data may need to be transformed from words to numbers. Then, you can use statistical analysis to answer your research questions.

Descriptive statistics will give you a summary of your data and include measures of averages and variability. You can also use graphs, scatter plots and frequency tables to visualize your data and check for any trends or outliers.

Using **inferential statistics**, you can make predictions or generalizations based on your data. You can test your hypothesis or use your sample data to estimate the population parameter.

Examples of descriptive and inferential statisticsYou hypothesize that first-year college students procrastinate more than fourth-year college students. You collect data on procrastination levels of the two groups using 7-point self-rating scales.

First, you use **descriptive statistics** to get a summary of the data. You find the mean (average) and the mode (most frequent rating) of procrastination of the two groups, and plot the data to see if there are any outliers.

Next, you perform **inferential statistics** to test your hypothesis. Using a t-test to compare the mean ratings of the two groups, you find a significant difference and support for your hypothesis.
You can also assess the reliability and validity of your data collection methods to indicate how consistently and accurately your methods actually measured what you wanted them to.

ADVANTAGES OF

QUANTITATIVE RESEARCH

Quantitative research is often used to standardize data collection and generalize findings. Strengths of this approach include:

- **Replication**

Repeating the study is possible because of standardized data collection protocols and tangible definitions of abstract concepts.

- **Direct comparisons of results**

The study can be reproduced in other cultural settings, times or with different groups of participants. Results can be compared statistically.

- **Large samples**

Data from large samples can be processed and analyzed using reliable and consistent procedures through quantitative data analysis.

- **Hypothesis testing**

Using formalized and established hypothesis testing procedures means that you have to carefully consider and report your research variables, predictions, data collection and testing methods before coming to a conclusion.

Disadvantages of quantitative research

Despite the benefits of quantitative research, it is sometimes inadequate in explaining complex research topics. Its limitations include:

- **Superficiality**

Using precise and restrictive operational definitions may inadequately represent complex concepts. For example, the concept of mood may be represented with just a number in quantitative research, but explained with elaboration in qualitative research.

- **Narrow focus**

Predetermined variables and measurement procedures can mean that you ignore other relevant observations.

- **Structural bias**

Despite standardized procedures, structural biases can still affect quantitative research. Missing data, imprecise measurements or inappropriate sampling methods are biases that can lead to the wrong conclusions.

- **Lack of context**

Quantitative research often uses unnatural settings like laboratories or fails to consider historical and cultural contexts that may affect data collection and results.

ANOTHER ON QUANTI....

Quantitative Research is a structured way of collecting and analyzing data obtained from different sources.
Quantitative Research involves the use of computational, statistical, and mathematical tools to derive results.

It is conclusive in its purpose as it tries to quantify the problem and understand how prevalent it is by looking for projectable results to a larger population.

On the other hand, qualitative research is generally more explorative, a type of research that is dependent on the collection of verbal, behavioral or observational data that can be interpreted in a subjective manner. It has a wide scope and is typically used to explore the causes of potential problems that may exist. Qualitative research typically provides insights on several aspects of a marketing problem. It often either precede or be conducted after quantitative research, depending on the study's objectives.

Companies who use quantitative research rather than qualitative are typically looking to measure extent and looking for statistical results that are interpreted objectively. While the results of qualitative research can vary according to the skills of observer, the results of quantitative research are interpreted in an almost similar manner by all experts.

Both types of research vary widely in not only their results, but all other aspects as well.

While qualitative data provides a subjective overview of marketing problems, quantitative defines a structured cause-and-effect relationship between the problem and factors.

One of the major differences in the two types of researches is the difference in the data collection method. Data collection is one of the most important aspects of the quantitative research process. Data collection involves having the researcher to prepare and obtain the required information from the target audience.

Data preparation includes determining the objective of data collection, methods of obtaining information, and the sequence of data collection activities. One of the most important aspect in this process is selecting the right sample for data collection. The data is then carefully collected from only those people who are most relevant to the objectives of the study. Known as a target segment, this sample is a group of people who are similar across a variety of variables.

The data collection tools for a quantitative research are surveys and experiments.
Experiments can provide specific results regarding the cause-and-effect relationship of several independent or interdependent factors related to a particular problem.

The most common approach to doing quantitative market research is a survey or questionnaire. Surveys can include interviews, which can be carried out using several different methodologies including face-to-face, telephone, online or computer assisted interviews.

After data collection, another step is the data analysis process.
The analysis of statistical data requires systematic tools and processes to be conducted. Many analytical

tools exist such as independent sample t-tests, correlated t-tests, variance calculations, and regression analysis that can be used to derive results from the data.

Now on QUALI....

8

MORE ON QUALITATIVE RESEARCH

According to Bhadari (2021) again, Qualitative research involves collecting and analyzing non-numerical data (e.g., text, video, or audio) to understand concepts, opinions, or experiences. It can be used to gather in-depth insights into a problem or generate new ideas for research.

Qualitative research is the opposite of quantitative research, which involves collecting and analyzing numerical data for statistical analysis.

Qualitative research is commonly used in the humanities and social sciences, in subjects such as anthropology, sociology, education, health sciences, history, etc.

Qualitative research question examples

- How does social media shape body image in teenagers?
- How do children and adults interpret healthy eating in the UK?
- What factors influence employee retention in a large organization?
- How is anxiety experienced around the world?
- How can teachers integrate social issues into science curriculums?

APPROACHES TO

QUALITATIVE RESEARCH

Qualitative research is used to understand how people experience the world. While there are many approaches to qualitative research, they tend to be flexible and focus on retaining rich meaning when

Qualitative research approaches

Approach	What does it involve?
Grounded theory	Researchers collect rich data on a topic of interest and develop theories inductively.
Ethnography	Researchers immerse themselves in groups or organizations to understand their cultures.
Action research	Researchers and participants collaboratively link theory to practice to drive social change.
Phenomenological research	Researchers investigate a phenomenon or event by describing and interpreting participants' lived experiences.
Narrative research	Researchers examine how stories are told to understand how participants perceive and make sense of their experiences.

interpreting data.

Common approaches include grounded theory, ethnography, action research, phenomenological research, and narrative research. They share some similarities, but emphasize different aims and perspectives.

Qualitative research methods

Each of the research approaches involve using one or more data collection methods. These are some of the most common qualitative methods:

- **Observations:** recording what you have seen, heard, or encountered in detailed field notes.
- **Interviews:** personally asking people questions in one-on-one conversations.
- **Focus groups:** asking questions and generating discussion among a group of people.
- **Surveys:** distributing questionnaires with open-ended questions.
- **Secondary research:** collecting existing data in the form of texts, images, audio or video recordings, etc.

Research exampleTo research the culture of a large tech company, you decide to take an ethnographic approach. You work at the company for several months and use various methods to gather data:

- You take field notes with observations and reflect on your own experiences of the company culture.
- You distribute open-ended surveys to employees across all the company's offices by

- email to find out if the culture varies across locations.
- You conduct in-depth interviews with employees in your office to learn about their experiences and perspectives in greater detail.

Qualitative researchers often consider themselves "instruments" in research because all observations, interpretations and analyses are filtered through their own personal lens.

For this reason, when writing up your methodology for qualitative research, it's important to reflect on your approach and to thoroughly explain the choices you made in collecting and analyzing the data.

What can proofreading do for your paper?

Scribbr editors not only correct grammar and spelling mistakes, but also strengthen your writing by making sure your paper is free of vague language, redundant words and awkward phrasing.

QUALITATIVE DATA ANALYSIS

Qualitative data can take the form of texts, photos, videos and audio. For example, you might be working with interview transcripts, survey responses, fieldnotes, or recordings from natural settings.

Most types of qualitative data analysis share the same five steps:

1. **Prepare and organize your data.** This may mean transcribing interviews or typing up fieldnotes.
2. **Review and explore your data.** Examine the data for patterns or repeated ideas that emerge.
3. **Develop a data coding system.** Based on your initial ideas, establish a set of codes that you can apply to categorize your data.
4. **Assign codes to the data.** For example, in qualitative survey analysis, this may mean going through each participant's responses and tagging them with codes in a spreadsheet. As you go through your data, you can create new codes to add to your system if necessary.
5. **Identify recurring themes.** Link codes together into cohesive, overarching themes.

There are several specific approaches to analyzing qualitative data. Although these methods share similar processes, they emphasize different concepts.

QUALITATIVE DATA ANALYSIS

Approach	**When to use**	**Example**
Content analysis	To describe and categorize common words, phrases, and	A market researcher could perform content analysis to find out what kind of

	ideas in qualitative data.	language is used in descriptions of therapeutic apps.
Thematic analysis	To identify and interpret patterns and themes in qualitative data.	A psychologist could apply thematic analysis to travel blogs to explore how tourism shapes self-identity.
Textual analysis	To examine the content, structure, and design of texts.	A media researcher could use textual analysis to understand how news coverage of celebrities has changed in the past decade.
Discourse analysis	To study communication and how language is used to achieve effects in specific contexts.	A political scientist could use discourse analysis to study how politicians generate trust in election campaigns.

ADVANTAGES OF

QUALITATIVE RESEARCH

Qualitative research often tries to preserve the voice and perspective of participants and can be adjusted as new research questions arise. Qualitative research is good for:

- **Flexibility**

The data collection and analysis process can be adapted as new ideas or patterns emerge. They are not rigidly decided beforehand.

- **Natural settings**

Data collection occurs in real-world contexts or in naturalistic ways.

- **Meaningful insights**

Detailed descriptions of people's experiences, feelings and perceptions can be used in designing, testing or improving systems or products.

- **Generation of new ideas**

Open-ended responses mean that researchers can uncover novel problems or opportunities that they wouldn't have thought of otherwise.

DISADVANTAGES OF

QUALITATIVE RESEARCH

Researchers must consider practical and theoretical limitations in analyzing and interpreting their data. Qualitative research suffers from:

- **Unreliability**

The real-world setting often makes qualitative research unreliable because of uncontrolled factors that affect the data.

- **Subjectivity**

Due to the researcher's primary role in analyzing and interpreting data, qualitative research cannot be replicated. The researcher decides what is important and what is irrelevant in data analysis, so interpretations of the same data can vary greatly.

- **Limited generalizability**

Small samples are often used to gather detailed data about specific contexts. Despite rigorous analysis procedures, it is difficult to draw generalizable conclusions because the data may be biased and unrepresentative of the wider population.

- **Labor-intensive**

Although software can be used to manage and record large amounts of text, data analysis often has to be checked or performed manually.

Additional....

As per the qualitative research definition, it is exploratory research that is used to understand the reasons and opinions of individuals. Moreover, it is an important market-based research study that focuses on obtaining qualitative data through open-ended conversations.

The purpose is to comprehend the main problem and develop ideas and methods for future quantitative research.

People typically use qualitative study in opposition to quantitative research. However, sometimes, they are not completely aware of the differences between qualitative vs. quantitative research. Many think that both serve the same purpose, which is not true.

Moreover, the methods of qualitative research have a long history in the field of social science. It is used to obtain and use qualitative data to understand the social life of the targeted population. Here, the primary focal point is the micro-level interaction.

megaphone Paper Due? Why suffer? That's our job! Click here to learn more.Types of Qualitative Research Methods

Researchers collect data of the targeted population, place, or event by using different types of qualitative research analysis.

COMMONLY USED QUALITATIVE RESEARCH TYPES

Below are the most commonly used qualitative research types for writing a research paper.

The following is a detailed description of these research types.

ETHNOGRAPHY METHOD

The table shows the basic elements of the ethnography method.

Purpose
Describe cultural characteristics

Method   I
dentify the cultural aspects and variables by reviewing the literatureGetting involved in the environment, live with the target audience, and collect data through observing and interacting with subjects

Analysis
Describe the main parameters of culture

Outcomes
A detailed description of the social morals

Ethnography is a branch of anthropology that provides the scientific explanation of human societies and cultures. It is one of the most popular and widely used techniques of qualitative research.

The fieldwork requires the researcher to get involved in the environment and live with the focus group. Such an interaction is done to understand the goals, motivations, challenges, and cultures of the individuals.

Similarly, it also helps to illustrate the cultural characteristics such as:

- ✓ Location
- ✓ Religion
- ✓ Tribal systems
- ✓ Shared experience
- ✓ Life style

Rather than conducting surveys and interviews, researchers experience the environment and act as an observer. Thus, the primary data collection method is observation over an extended period.

However, it would also be appropriate to interview those who have studied the same cultures.

Ethnographic research becomes difficult if the researcher is not familiar with the social morals and language of the group. Furthermore, interpretations by outsiders may also lead to confusion.

Thus, it requires the researcher to validate the data before presenting the findings.

For Example:

A good approach to understand the needs of the customers is by observing their daily activities. Notice how they interact with the product.

For this, you don't have to come up with any hypotheses to test. However, you only need it in the social life of the subjects.

NARRATIVE METHOD

Have a look at the table given below.

Narrative Method

Purpose
Collect data in the form of a cohesive story

Method
Review the sequence of events, and conduct interviews to describe the largest influences that affected an individual.

Analysis
Analyze different life situations and opportunities

Outcomes

Present a short story with themes, conflicts, and challenges
The narrative research method occurs over a long period for compiling the data. It takes a sequence of events to form a cohesive story. However, similar to a story narrative, it takes a subject from a starting point and reviews different situations of life.

Here, the researcher conducts in-depth interviews and reads various documents. Moreover, it also reviews the events that largely impact the personality of an individual.

Sometimes, interviews are conducted even after weeks, months, or years. Nevertheless, this method requires the outcomes to be presented in a short story with themes.

It may also include the conflicts, tensions, and challenges that have become a great opportunity for innovation.

For Example:

The narrative method can be used in a business to understand the different challenges faced by the target audience. Moreover, it can be utilized for further innovation and development of products.

PHENOMENOLOGICAL METHOD

The following are the essential aspects of this research method.

Phenomenological Method

Purpose
Describe the experiences, events, or situations from different angles

Method
Sampling and data collection by conducting interviews, observation, surveys, and reading documentsDescribe and write the experience of the phenomena

Data Analysis
Classify the data and examine the experiences beyond human awareness

Outcomes
A database is formed to describe the findings from a subject's viewpoint

The word phenomenological means the study of a phenomenon such as events, situations, or experiences. It is the best approach to describe something from different angles and add to the existing knowledge. Similarly, it focuses on subjective experiences.

Here, a researcher uses different methods to gather data and understand the phenomenon. These methods include interviews, visiting places, observation, surveys, and reading documents.

Lastly, this technique takes into account how participants feel about things during an event or activity. Thus, a database with themes is formed to validate the findings.

For Example:

You can use this method to understand why students prefer to take online courses. Moreover, it will also identify the reason behind the rise in the number of students from the last few years.

GROUNDED THEORY METHOD

Check out the table below to understand the elements of a grounded theory method.

Grounded Theory Method

Purpose
Used to develop theory, identify social development and ways to deal itInvolves the formulation and testing of data until the theory is developed

Method
Data collection methods such as interviews, observation, literature review, and document analysis

Analysis
Theory formation and development by a sampling of literature

Outcomes
Theory supported by relevant examples from data

A phenomenological study describes an event. Whereas, a grounded theory approach provides an explanation, reasons, or theory behind that event. It aims to develop new theories by collecting and analyzing data about a phenomenon.

Here, a researcher makes use of various data collection techniques. It includes observation, interview, literature review, and relevant document analysis. Moreover, the unit of content analysis is a specific phenomenon or incident and not individual behaviors.

Usually, different coding techniques and large sample sizes are used to identify themes and develop a better theory.

For Example:

This method can be used in businesses to conduct surveys. It also helps to demonstrate why the consumer uses the company's product or services.

The data collected through these surveys help companies to improve and maintain their customer's satisfaction and loyalty.

CASE STUDY

Here are the main characteristics of a case study method.

Case Study

Purpose
Describe an experience, person, event, or place in detail

Method
Direct observation and interaction with the subject

Analysis
Analyze the experiences

Outcomes
An in-depth description of the subjects

The case study approach occurs over extended periods of time to compile information. It involves an in-depth understanding of a subject such as an event, person, business, or place.

Similarly, the data is collected from various sources, including interviews, direct observation, and historical documentation.

Case studies are carried out in different disciplines like law, education, medicine, and sciences. Therefore, they can be descriptive or explanatory in nature.

Furthermore, this method is used when the researcher wants to focus on:

'How' and 'why' research questionsThe behaviors under observationUnderstand the phenomenonThe context of the phenomena

For Example:

Businesses can use case studies to show their business solutions effectively. Similarly, it also helps them to identify how they can solve a particular problem for the subject.

Let suppose a company AB introduces new UX designs into an agile environment. It would be considered as enlightening to many companies.

HISTORICAL METHOD

Have a look at the below table to understand the historical method.

Historical Method

Purpose
Describe and examines past events to understand present patterns and predicting future scenarios

Method
Develop your idea after reading the relevant literature
Develop the types of qualitative research questions
Identify the sources - archives, libraries, papers

Clarify the reliability and validity of data sources
Create a research outline to organize the process
Collect data

Analysis
Analyze the data by accepting or rejecting it
Identify the conflicting evidence

Outcomes
Present the findings in the form of biography or paper

The historical method describes past events to understand present scenarios and predict future choices. It answers the research questions based on a hypothetical idea. Later this technique used multiple resources to test the idea for any potential challenges.

It also requires the development of the research outline to organize the whole process. Lastly, the historical method presents the findings in the form of a biography.

For Example:

For creating new ads, businesses can use historical data of previous ad campaigns and the targeted demographics.

TYPES OF QUALITATIVE RESEARCH DESIGN EXAMPLES

Types of Qualitative Research Design Examples (PDF) If you are assigned to submit a qualitative research paper soon, the above guide will help you.

Here, different types of qualitative research methodology can assist in understanding the behavior and motivations of people. Similarly, it will also help in generating original ideas and formulate a better research problem.

However, not everyone can write a good research paper. Thus, if you get stuck at any stage of writing your qualitative research paper, you can take professional help.

MyPerfectWords.com is the best paper writing service, where you can get a professional writer. They have the expertise and advanced degrees from U.S. based institutes.

Similarly, we will help you to use different qualitative examples and methods to write your research paper. However, if you are still confused about trusting us, check out the paper samples and customer reviews on our website.

We assure that you will receive a high-quality paper at the most reasonable rates. Simply contact our writing team now and place your order.

9

STEP BY STEP

Research Paper Definition

A research paper is an expanded essay that contains a detailed analysis and interpretation of the argument. It also involves an in-depth survey of a field of knowledge for finding the best possible information.

A research paper can be defined as a type of academic writing that is usually done as a class assignment. Similarly, it requires the writer to conduct independent research and writing on a topic in a scientific manner.

Types of Research

Below are the two main types of research.

- Qualitative research
- Quantitative research

HOW TO START A RESEARCH PAPER?

A good research paper must follow a proper structure and format. The first important step inthe writing process is to start your paper perfectly.

To start a research paper, follow the below steps.

1. Read the guidelines to start early
2. Brainstorm to choose a research paper topic
3. Conduct research and find relevant material
4. Organize your research and prepare an outline
5. Create a strong thesis statement
6. Start from the main body

It is important to know about the steps involved in starting and writing the research paper. It will be a big help in your writing process. Continue reading to learn more about successful techniques to make this process as effective as possible.

How to Write a Research Paper?

To write a research paper, follow the steps given below.

Understand the Paper Requirements

The first step requires a proper and thorough understanding of the assigned topic and research paper structure. It will help you complete the assignment successfully and easily by following all the requirements.

Below are the tips to develop your understanding of the research paper:

- Read the instructions carefully. If you find something confusing, clarify it with your professor right away.
- Understand the main purpose of the research paper. It may include informing people or encouraging them to take a certain course of action.
- Also, identify the deadline, word count, submission method, and formatting style.
- Make a list of the key points that you need to cover.
- Consider the timeframe to start, write, and edit your research paper.

Consider the Target Audience

Considering the target audience is the most crucial step while writing a paper. It is because their knowledge and expertise level can influence the following elements:

- The author's writing style
- Word choice
- The type of relevant information required to explain the concept

A master's level research paper is usually written for the expert audience. However, if you are writing an undergraduate paper, it can be both for a general and expert audience.

Choose the Right Research Paper Topic

Brainstorm ideas to choose the right topic for your research paper. Most students are often assigned to their topics. Nevertheless, if you are given the opportunity to choose a topic yourself, choose it wisely.

Discuss with your professor or a subject specialist to figure out a unique approach. Moreover, try freewriting that can help in narrowing down a broad topic.

Apart from this, you can also get inspiration from other research work. Some research papers include ideas for other topics in their discussion and recommendation sections.

Think of something challenging that will interest your audience as well. It will help you stay engaged while conducting research as you are sure to discover new things and enlighten your audience with new information.

Similarly, don't select too technical or general topics. Instead, choose an original and specific idea that is possible to research. Also, keep in mind and stay focused on the criteria of your research paper while selecting a topic.

Here are some amazing research paper topics.

- Can different generations work in the same place?
- Can social media marketing help to improve the brand image?

- The creation of particular learning methods for blind children.
- A link between mental health and child obesity.
- The death sentence should be activated in every country of the world.

If you need more ideas, we have compiled a list of good research paper topics to help you choose one for your paper.

We have also divided these topics into different categories like education, law, health, or psychology research topics for your ease.

Conduct Thorough Research

A writer should conduct thorough research to find relevant ideas, focus, and direction to the topic. Use credible sources such as journals, books, and official websites to gather the data. These will help in supporting your viewpoint and avoiding any biases.

Also, address the below questions.

- Is there a gap in the previous research work?
- Are there any recent developments in your chosen subject?
- Are there any headed debates going on that you can address?
- Do you have a unique perspective on the topic to talk about?

Here you can develop your research questions and a strong argument for your paper. Similarly, you can also determine any possible flaws or adjustments in the topic.

Develop a Strong Thesis Statement

After conducting the research, the next step is to develop a strong thesis statement. It serves as a central argument that establishes the purpose and position of your research paper. Also, provide solid evidence and reasoning to support your thesis statement.

Similarly, a research paper thesis should be concise, clear, and to the point. This two-line sentence is considered as a guide throughout the writing process. A writer can further do more research to revise it.

Refer to the below documents to write a perfect thesis statement.

HOW TO WRITE A THESIS FOR A RESEARCH PAPER

Preparing a Research Paper Proposal

A research proposal aims to explain the need to analyze a research problem by considering more realistic approaches. An in-depth literature review plays an important role in creating a good research proposal.

Here are some questions you should address while writing a research proposal.

- What are you planning to accomplish?
- Why do you want to accomplish it?
- How will you plan to approach or accomplish it?

With these questions, a writer will be able to plan and prepare a research study. Similarly, a research proposal must include the following sections.

1. Title page
2. Abstract and table of contents
3. Introduction
4. Background and significance
5. Literature review
6. Research design and methods
7. Hypothesis and discussion
8. Conclusion
9. Citations

Create a Research Paper Outline

Create a detailed outline to organize all your thoughts in one place. It serves as a mind map or layout of your writing process. Similarly, it is also used to plan the paper before even starting to write it.

It consists of the key topics, arguments, and evidence that will be included in the sections of your paper. Thus, take enough time to create a well-structured outline.

Below given are the components of an effective research paper outline.

1. Title Page
2. Abstract
3. Table of Contents
4. Introduction
5. Body
6. Literature Review
7. Methods
8. Results
9. Discussion
10. Conclusion
11. Bibliography
12. Appendix

Writing the First Draft

Write the first draft of your research paper. You can polish this section later on. Here the main goal is to:

- Draft rough ideas into arguments.
- Add details to the arguments.
- See how the final outcome will look like.
- Follow a proper research paper format.
- Pay close attention to the organization of the paragraphs and sentences.
- Explain the ideas and the significance of your findings clearly.
- Keeping the arguments flexible so that they can be changed later if needed.
- Do proper citation.

Remember, it is not necessary to write the introduction first. Some writers prefer to write the difficult sections first while others choose to start with the easiest one. Use your outline as a map to guide you throughout the different parts of a research paper.

Write an Abstract

The abstract of the research paper is the summary of the entire paper. When writing one, explain each section of your paper briefly and highlight the main points that you are going to discuss.

Keep in mind that the abstract should not be more than 250 words or less than 150 words. It roughly makes almost half of a page. Thus, keep a strict check on word choice and count.

WRITE A RESEARCH PAPER INTRODUCTION

The introduction of a research paper should address 'What', 'Why', and 'How' questions. It should be concise and without any arguments. The reader must be able to answer what the paper is about after reading this section.

Below is a detailed description of the questions.

- **What?** Be specific about the topic. Introduce historical background and define difficult terms and theories.

- **Why?** It is the most important part of an introduction. It aims to discuss any new insights you are offering with your research study.

- **How?** This section will tell the audience about how your paper will proceed. Thus, it should present all the main elements that will be discussed in your research work.

CRAFTING A PERFECT LITERATURE REVIEW

After the introduction, the next part of the research paper is the literature review. Here, a writer needs to discuss the existing literature about the research problem.

For this, try to locate scholarly or peer-reviewed research articles on the same topic. Study it thoroughly and highlight the similarities between the research article and your study.

Discuss the past, the present state, and the expected future of the issue in your literature review section. Also, provide a detailed insight into the previously conducted research in the field.

You can also refer to our blog to learn how to write a literature review.

DRAFTING THE RESEARCH PAPER BODY PARAGRAPHS

Use the research paper outline as a guide to draft your body paragraphs. It will help you present the information, supporting details, and arguments logically.

The main element is to stay on track by using the thesis statement. Provide strong evidence and examples to support the main idea.

Moreover, each paragraph should start with a compelling topic sentence and include no more than a single idea. Also, look for smooth transitions between the body paragraphs.

WRITING A RESEARCH PAPER CONCLUSION

The conclusion is the last section of your writing draft that gives a sense of closure. It will provide a brief summary of the entire paper. Similarly, also mention how you have proved your main idea by using the research questions.

Nevertheless, do not introduce new arguments or information that may leave an open-ended question in the minds of the audience. But you can suggest a possible course of action or prospects for future research to conclude your research paper.

Lastly, a writer should also avoid adding unnecessary details to increase the word count only.

Write the Second Draft

After roughly organizing your thoughts in the first draft, begin writing the second draft of your paper. Keep in mind the below aspects to write a second draft perfectly.

- Ensure if you have answered the main argument effectively.
- Identify any assumptions that you may require to include.
- Rearrange and structure the ideas logically.
- If you find any old and irrelevant ideas, cut them out. Instead, add new and unique approaches.
- Make a work cited list.

Revising and Proofreading

Revising and proofreading is the last step of your writing process. It is done to ensure that the paper is well-developed and free of mistakes.

Similarly, it is also used to confirm the following points of your paper:

- If the paper has met all the requirements?
- Check for the logical order of paragraphs.
- No irrelevant details should be there.
- Look for grammatical, punctuation, and spelling mistakes.
- Identify wrong sentence structures.
- Check for consistency with the font, headings, page numbers, and format.

- Make sure that all sources are properly referenced by using a specific citation style guide.

You can proofread your research paper by reading it aloud. it will help you consider each word more closely. Moreover, you can also hire someone to proofread it for you.

Read the document given below to get a better understanding of writing a research paper.

Research Paper Examples

You will be able to work on your research paper without any difficulty after reading this blog. However, if you are still confused about how to do a research paper, explore the research paper examples to learn more.

Hire an Expert Writer for Your Research Paper!

The above-mentioned complete guide will help you write a perfect research paper. However, we understand that it is quite difficult for students who lack good writing and research skills.

In such a case, academic and professional writing companies are proved to be helpful. It is a common practice and indeed a smart thing to do.

Though it is challenging to find a legit writing company that can provide help at affordable rates. Below are the attributes of a reliable writing service.

- Plagiarism free work
- Free essay and paper samples
- U.S-based qualified writers
- Direct contact with the writer
- Able to meet a strict deadline
- Secure and confidential payment system
- Free and unlimited revisions

10

Research Paper

Do you spend time staring at the screen and thinking about how to approach a monstrous research paper?

If yes, you are not alone.

Research papers are no less than a curse for high school and college students.

It takes time, effort, and expertise to craft a striking research paper.

Every other person craves to master the magic of producing impressive research papers.

Continue with the guide to investigate the mysterious nature of different types of research through examples.

Diverse Research Paper Examples

Research papers are not limited to a specific field.

Coping with the diversity in research papers remains a tough nut to crack.

See-through the list where we've offered examples on several subjects.

Example of Abstract

After submitting the research proposal, prepare for writing a seasoned abstract section. The abstract delivers the bigger picture by revealing the purpose of the research.

A common mistake made by students is writing it the same way a summary is written.

Remember!

It is not merely a summary but an analysis of the whole research project.

Task:

Copy an abstract here and dissect its component parts.

Scientific Research Paper

We have discussed several elements of research papers through examples.

Abstract!

Research Proposal!

Introduction in Research Paper!

Read on to move towards advanced versions of information.

Scientific research paper

Let's have a look at the template and an example to elaborate concepts.

It includes:

- Abstract
- Introduction
- Related Work
- Methodologies
- Experiments
- Results and Discussion
- Conclusion & Future Work
- Acknowledgment
- References

The name itself sounds terrifying to many students. Make no mistake; it sure is dangerous when touched without practice.

Students become afraid and hence aspire to locate an outstanding essay paper writer to get their papers done.

Detailed, high-quality, and credible sources and samples are a must to be shared here.

METHODOLOGY IN RESEARCH PAPER

The words methodology, procedure, and approach are the same. They indicate the approach pursued by the researcher while conducting research to accomplish the goal through research.

The methodology is the bloodline of the research paper.

A practical or assumed procedure is used to conduct methodology.

Research Paper Outline Example

Before you plan on writing a well-researched paper, make a rough draft.

Brainstorm again and again!

Pour all of your ideas in the basket of the outline.

What will it include?

This example outlines the following elements:

- Introduction
- Thesis Statement
- Main Idea
- Sub Idea
- Methodology
- Conclusion

Utilize this standard of outline in your research papers to polish your paper. Here is a step by step guide that will help you write a research paper according to this format.

LITERATURE REVIEW

What if a novice person reads your research paper?

He will never understand the critical elements involved in the research paper.

To enlighten him, focus on the literature review section. This section offers an extensive analysis of the past research conducted on the paper topics.

It is relatively easier than other sections of the paper.

How?

Take a closer look at the paper below to find out.

METHODS SECTION OF RESEARCH PAPER

While writing research papers, excellent papers focus a great deal on the methodology.

Yes, the research sample and methodology define the fate of the papers.

Are you facing the trouble going through the methodology section?

Relax and let comprehensive sample research papers clear your doubts.

GOOD RESEARCH PAPER

Theoretically, good research paper examples will meet the objectives of the research.

Always remember! The first goal of the research paper is to explain ideas, goals, and theory as clear as water.

Yes, leave no room for confusion of any sort.

When the professor reads such a professional research paper, he will be delighted.

High scores!

Grant of funds for the project!

Appreciation in Class!

You'll surely be highly rewarded.

RESEARCH PAPER CONCLUSION

The conclusion leaves the last impression on the reader.

"Who cares for the last impression? It's always the first."

Don't be fooled!

The conclusion sets the tone of the whole research paper properly.

A key list of elements must be present in the conclusion to make it crisp and remarkable.

CRITICAL RESEARCH PAPER

To write a research paper remarkably, include the following ingredients in it:

- Justification of the Experimental Design
- Analysis of Results
- Validation of the Study

THEORETICAL FRAMEWORK EXAMPLES

The theoretical framework is the key to establish credibility in research papers.

Read the purpose of the theoretical framework before following it in the research paper.

The researcher offers a guide through a theoretical framework.

- Philosophical view
- Conceptual Analysis
- Benefits of the Research

An in-depth analysis of theoretical framework examples research paper is underlined in the sample below.

11

RESEARCH PAPER OUTLINE

What Is A Research Paper Outline?

A research paper outline is basically a blueprint for a complete subject. It serves as a mindmap and a plan of action that most students follow throughout the writing process.

The following are the benefits of creating a well-structured outline.

- Organizes all the thoughts and ideas in one place.
- Provides a detailed structure for your future research work.
- Demonstrates your understanding and vision of a particular topic.
- Avoids any possible mistakes by shaping a topic.
- Helps not to skip any important points.
- Gives an idea for the future headings of the paper.
- Understanding the flow of information and how ideas are related.
- Gives the audience a clear idea of what is included in the paper.

How to Write a Research Paper Outline?

The following is a detailed explanation of the steps to write a college research paper outline.

Cover or Title page

It should contain the title of the paper written within 60 characters. Similarly, it also includes:

- Student's full name
- Name of the instructor
- Course title and code
- Submission date

Abstract

The abstract briefly summarize your paper by stating the basic information in five to six sentences. Moreover, this section comes after the title page and mainly focuses on:

- The main arguments
- The research methods
- The subject matter
- Participants
- Outcomes

Make sure the abstract should not exceed the ⅓ of the page i.e. about 150 to 200 words.

You can also take help from our detailed guide about writing a research paper abstract.

Table of Contents

The table of contents will summarize the chapters and sections in an organized manner. Furthermore, it also includes the title and descriptions of the headings and subheadings.

This section provides readers with a complete overview of the document's contents. Also, it allows them to go directly to a specific section of the research paper.

Research Paper Introduction

The introduction is the most important part of any research paper. It should be able to present the topic and answer the research question. Similarly, it will also explain the importance of the subject matter for the audience.

The central aim is to grab the reader's attention with the help of strong arguments. Thus, this section must be engaging and interesting enough.

Below are the four main elements to write a compelling introduction:

- **A Hook -** An engaging start to persuade the readers to read more. It is about 1 to 2 sentences in length.

- **Background Information** - Present the historical background of the topic along with the general information for better understanding.
- **A Thesis Statement** - It explains the major points of your paper that discusses why the topic is of great importance. Thus, it must be clear, specific, and to the point.
- **Define The Audience** - Understand and define your target audience. Explain the reasons why they are interested in reading your content.

Research Paper Body

The body is the main section of your research paper. It consists of several paragraphs that include the relevant details, examples, and evidence to support your argument.

Moreover, you can also provide counterarguments and opposing facts. Such factors help the reader to get an idea about your understanding of the topic.

Make sure the paper should remain consistent from the beginning to the end. The style, tone, and citation should be according to the required format.

Literature Review

This section will mention the literature that you have used to support your hypothesis and theories. Demonstrate the research gaps in the existing literature. Also, show how it helped you to research and find relevant data and develop your research.

Related: Learn How to Write a Literature Review in Simple Steps

Method

Here, you will present the techniques and types of equipment that you have employed to carry out the research work. Keep in mind that the methods can vary according to the subject matter.

Therefore, you need to give a detailed explanation of how you have conducted the research.

Results

A good research paper is the one that has facts and figures to justify the argument. In this section, you will focus on the findings of your paper. Make sure to add as many facts, statistics, and numbers as possible.

Use tables and graphs to be more precise and structured. Remember to tell the audience how the outcome has contributed to the field of study as a whole.

Discussion

Most students get confused between the Results and Discussion. There is a simple line that separates both.

Results focus on facts and figures. However, in the discussion section, a writer makes sure whether the expected results are achieved or not.

Research Paper Conclusion

The conclusion is the final part of your research work that summarizes the main arguments. Similarly, it also restates the thesis, goals, and methods that are used to achieve the results.

There is no need to provide a detailed explanation. Instead, just give a general overview. Also, formulate the prospect for future research and a call to action to provoke the readers.

However, the conclusion should not be longer than the abstract.

Bibliography and Appendix

Lastly, mention all the sources that you have used in your text. Do not forget any references in the bibliography section.

Also, add facts, tables, images, and charts in the section of the Appendix. Nevertheless, in some formats, the appendix is not required at all.

RESEARCH PAPER OUTLINE FORMAT

Choosing a format is important to develop an outline. As it will help you organize the information in a specific way.

Every college uses a specific format to structure or outlining the major ideas of the paper. So it is obvious that the APA format paper will be different from the MLA format.

Create a list of elements for your paper and properly section them into categories. You can even label each part in Roman numerals for easy understanding.

Below is the detailed description of two commonly used outline formats.

MLA Format Outline

The research paper outline according to MLA format includes the following elements.

1. The student and professor's name, class, and date appear on the first page.
2. The header contains the page numbers at the upper right corner.
3. All titles to be written in italics.
4. A complete list with endnotes before cited works.
5. Subheadings are written with Arabic numerals.

APA Format Outline

Here are the main characteristics of the APA research paper outline.

1. It must include a separate cover page.
2. The cover page features the title, name of the author, university, and running head.
3. The header contains page numbers and the title of the paper.
4. APA format usually requires to include Abstract.
5. A list of cited sources entitled "References."

Similarly, it is of great help to follow an example. Thus, you can further go through the outline examples in APA and MLA format by reviewing the research paper examples.

STANDARD RESEARCH PAPER OUTLINE FORMAT

The following is the standard research paper outline format. It is the basis for creating a successful, more detailed, and high-quality research paper.

Introduction

- Hook statement.
- Define the audience.
- A strong Thesis statement.

Body Paragraphs

- Arguments to support your thesis statement.

Conclusion

- Summary of arguments.
- Call to action.

Below is a template for a standard research paper outline.

HIRE A PROFESSIONAL WRITER

The above guide will help you to start writing an outline for your research paper. However, there are students who lack good writing skills and prefer to seek professional help.

But, this is also where a lot of people get into trouble. In a hurry to meet the deadline, they end up ordering from an unreliable paper writing service.

Thus, it is important to understand that a high-quality research paper takes time and proper research.

12

Research Paper Topics

There are a number of tasks you will have to face when you enroll in a college. Most students feel stressed and tired, particularly when it comes to writing a research paper.

Some say the hardest part of drafting a text is to get started. However, selecting good research topics even precedes the starting point. This practice takes a lot of time and creativity. Therefore, by exploring this complete guide, you will get plenty of topic ideas in no time.

Most of the time, the instructors assign the list of topics to the students. While, sometimes, they give you the freedom to come up with the topic of your choice.

This is where our list of best research paper topics will come in handy. The essay experts at MyPerfectWords.com have collected impressive ideas for your paper. We will assist you in turning an average research paper into an exceptional one.

HOW TO FIND A GOOD RESEARCH PAPER TOPIC?

There are some other special techniques that you should follow to pick the right research paper topic. Follow the easy steps below to find good research paper topics.

Conduct Background Research

The first step is to conduct detailed background research by reviewing the existing literature. It will help to identify the history of a well-defined research problem. Similarly, it will also assist in developing research questions and a thesis statement.

Brainstorm Topic Ideas

Brainstorm research topic ideas and make a list of the general subjects. Narrow down to a specific field of study and choose the one that interests you the most. It is the key to produce an interesting and impressive writing piece.

You can further take help from your professor to identify a unique idea to write a research paper. Remember, it would be better to avoid controversial topics for research papers if you are not confident about justifying them.

Find Relevant Information

The next step is to find relevant information about your chosen topic. For this, read different points of view available on the internet. Also, consult scholarly sources like books and peer-reviewed articles to keep the facts straight and referable.

Use Keywords

Try to come up with a keyword and reach the best-suited topic according to your subject and preference. For example, the keyword 'violence' can provide you with a number of choices. It may include gun violence, domestic violence, and other essay topics related to abuse.

This step serves as a crucial strategy to grab the reader's attention.

Keep Your Audience in Mind

Always keep your target audience in mind. It is another important element in selecting your high-school or college research paper topics.

For this, a writer strictly needs to comply with the instructor's preference and requirements. Make sure your topic gets approved before you begin with the writing process.

Here are some impressive and easy research paper topics to write an extraordinary paper.

Research Paper Topics on Marketing and Business

- ✓ Explain workforce rules and regulations in Manila
- ✓ How can we stop corporate abuse?
- ✓ Small business innovations to grow your business setup.
- ✓ Ways to reduce taxes in small businesses.
- ✓ Effective tips for women in business.
- ✓ How has marketing etiquette changed in the last few years?
- ✓ Why are stock markets becoming more popular?
- ✓ What are the positive effects of relationship marketing?
- ✓ How globalization impacts brand marketing?
- ✓ Can women prove to be better marketing experts than men?

Research Paper Topics on Economics

- ✓ Discuss Balanced vs. Unbalanced growth.
- ✓ How to improve the quality of life in developing countries?
- ✓ Ways to measure and manage inflation.

- ✓ Demand and supply analysis – A complete guide
- ✓ History trends in Income disparity.
- ✓ An easy guideline for property rights.
- ✓ Standards versus taxes as policy instruments.
- ✓ Explain the difference between private and public finance.
- ✓ Understanding the dynamics of economics and culture influence.
- ✓ Immigration and its impacts on the economy

Research Paper Topics on Current Affairs

- ✓ How has feminism changed over the years?
- ✓ Has the "Black Lives Matter" movement reduced racism in the United States?
- ✓ Are we moving towards World War 3?
- ✓ Has China decided to tackle its pollution problem?
- ✓ India: A poor nation or a superpower?
- ✓ Is the Philippine economy becoming stronger or weaker?
- ✓ How important is it to reduce the Federal budget deficit?
- ✓ How can police departments minimize the danger to officers from shooters?
- ✓ How can Manila reduce the amount of violence and murders in the city?
- ✓ Should it be easier for people to become United States citizens?

Research Paper Topics on Education

- ✓ Should Filipino students take a gap year between school and college?
- ✓ Discuss the concept of homeschool along with its benefits.
- ✓ Education and funding - A complete overview.
- ✓ Pros and cons of standardized tests - Discuss briefly.
- ✓ Do college students make more money?
- ✓ Should education be cheaper?
- ✓ How will modern technologies change the way of teaching in the future?
- ✓ The creation of particular learning methods for blind children.
- ✓ Benefits and risks of social networking in school.
- ✓ The role of technology in lesson planning.

Research Paper Topics on English Literature

- ✓ Similarities and differences between Shakespeare and Charles Dickens.
- ✓ Do you believe that Dickens failed after turning to serious and romantic novels?
- ✓ Examine controversies associated with Shakespeare
- ✓ .Literature as an instrument of propaganda.
- ✓ The American Dream in the 20th century's literature.
- ✓ Religion and literature in a secular age.
- ✓ Discuss the works of Hemingway.

- ✓ Why did "Harry Potter" become so popular?
- ✓ Classify artificial languages in literature.
- ✓ What is the role of mythology in English literature?

Psychology Research Paper Topics

- ✓ Causes of depression among youth.
- ✓ Define Memory and its types.Why do we dream?
- ✓ Criminal psychology vs. Forensic psychology.
- ✓ Child abuse - Ways to prevent it.
- ✓ The relation between obesity and watching TV
- ✓ .Discuss the psychological reasons for mental stress.
- ✓ Elaborate on the link between mental health and child obesity.
- ✓ Are later mental health issues related to childhood trauma?

Research Paper Topics on Bullying

- ✓ Top punishments for bullying.
- ✓ Cyberbullying and how to stop it.
- ✓ Types and consequences of Individual bullying.
- ✓ Should laws be enforced to stop bullying?
- ✓ Can bullying be a cause for murder?
- ✓ What should school authorities do to fight to bully?
- ✓ How to identify and manage workplace bullying?
- ✓ What does it feel like to be bullied?

- ✓ Do bullies specifically choose their targets in school?
- ✓ Do people abandon unwanted behavior when they graduate school?

Research Paper Topics on Culture

- ✓ Explore the evolution of rap music.
- ✓ Is Ethnic conflict avoidable?
- ✓ Does religion influence culture and to what extent?
- ✓ How different cultures deal with deaths?
- ✓ Culture of my community - A detailed overview
- ✓ Gender roles in different cultures - A cross-cultural perspective.
- ✓ Discuss the History of cultural revolutions.
- ✓ 10 most prominent cultural events of the 20th century.
- ✓ Struggles of Interracial Relationships
- ✓ The power of Mentoring minorities in the workplace.

Research Paper Topics on Arts

Differences in the Italian Renaissance and Northern Renaissance.Impacts famous artists had on the world.Explain the art of Ancient Egypt.Art therapy is used to heal people. How?Is photography an art?Discuss the history of the Bauhaus Movement.Discuss the concept of censorship in art.Digital art and its rise.Hollywood vs. Bollywood.Fine art vs. Folk art.

Easy Research Paper Topics

- ✓ Steps involved in making a music video?
- ✓ Discuss the factors that can stop sexual harassment.
- ✓ The negative impacts of feminism on the employment culture.
- ✓ How to deal with personality orders?
- ✓ Why white-collar jobs losing their significance?
- ✓ Discuss the consequences of homeschooling.
- ✓ Effects of using plastic bags.
- ✓ How to solve the issue of gender discrimination at workplaces?
- ✓ Factors that can influence the behavior of an individual.
- ✓ Impacts of social networks on mental health

Research Paper Topics on World Problems

- ✓ Discuss the examples of human rights violations.
- ✓ Consequences of the shortage of natural resources.
- ✓ What is the difference between global warming and climate change?
- ✓ he crisis of water pollution and shortage.
- ✓ Violence and Conflict Resolution in the changing world order.

- ✓ World Trade and Tourism - A global agenda for sustainable development.
- ✓ How can we overcome the challenge of corruption in governance
- ✓ Discuss the brief history of space exploration.
- ✓ What are the effects of migration on the urban population?
- ✓ Discuss top wild animals' endangered species.

Research Paper Topics on Crime and Law

- ✓ Should the police use body cameras?
- ✓ What is White-collar crime? Discuss examples.
- ✓ Penalties for DUI (Drinking Under the Influence) should be made stricter. Why?
- ✓ Discuss laws that protect animal rights.10 facts about hate crimes.
- ✓ Causes of Sexual harassment in the workplace.
- ✓ What action should the government take to address police brutality?
- ✓ Ethics of Assisted suicide.
- ✓ Is it possible to cure a serial killer?
- ✓ What can we do to curb domestic violence?

Funny Research Paper Topics

- ✓ How companies can improve their odds by becoming a unicorn?
- ✓ Pop art vs. lady gaga.
- ✓ The art of erasing bad memories and only remembering good ones.

- ✓ Can chicken feathers determine the speed of tornados?
- ✓ Harry Potter and the world of wizards
- ✓ Do You Love Using Your Surname?
- ✓ Why Do Most People Love Watching Funny Animal Videos?
- ✓ Do You Know What Your Pet Dog Is Thinking?
- ✓ All Men Know How To Pick The Right Clothes.
- ✓ School Dropouts Are The Best In Our Society.

The above given interesting research topics will help you write a perfect research paper.

If you still need more good ideas, seeking essay writing help is what most students prefer.

Keep in mind, the writing industry has a lot of fake and inexperienced writers. And if you're not careful you might be scammed easily. So while choosing a paper writing service, you need to be very careful.

Similarly, most companies do not hire subject specialists with advanced knowledge and expertise. This is where MyPerfectWords.com comes in.

Our professionals have Masters and PhD degrees. We work with an aim to provide 100% original and high-quality papers.

Similarly, our company makes sure to assign a subject specialist to work on your research paper at affordable rates. We will not only select research paper topics ideas for you but will also assist in writing your paper from scratch.

Simply, place your order now to work with our expert writers and get your paper done.

13

Research Proposal

Academic assignments involving research work usually haunt students. A research proposal is a first and integral step in writing a research paper. It is considered as a complex task because it requires multiple skills and a critical approach.

Similarly, a good research proposal must contain the contribution of the research work to a particular field of study. It should also include why and how a research study is useful for the society and the audience.

If you deliver an ordinary proposal, you are more likely to get a low score. Thus, make sure you invest all the time and energy to draft a strong proposal.

This guide offers a comprehensive outlook of the steps required to write a winning research project proposal.

WHAT IS A RESEARCH PROPOSAL?

As per the research proposal definition, it is a concise summary of the entire study and the main research questions. It is also used to describe what you will inquire about why it is important, and how you will conduct the research work.

Similarly, a good proposal also identifies the knowledge of existing literature and suggests practical solutions. Here you will explain the nature and significance of the research study to persuade the audience.

PURPOSE OF A

RESEARCH PROPOSAL

Below given are the purposes of making a research proposal.

- It is crucial for academics to get funding for their projects.
- Students get their thesis and dissertation plan approved.
- It convinces the audience about the importance of a research study.
- It shows the writer's in-depth understanding of a particular field.
- It also makes a case for your research methodology to collect data.
- It polishes the research and critical thinking skills.

- It also identifies the logical steps that need to be taken to achieve the goals.
- It analyzes the data to address the research problem.

HOW LONG IS A RESEARCH PROPOSAL?

The length of a proposal varies in different course programs. It consists of only a few pages for writing a bachelor's or master's thesis proposal. However, the proposals for PhD dissertations are long and detailed.

HOW TO WRITE A RESEARCH PROPOSAL?

To write a research proposal, a writer must answer the following questions.

- **What are you planning to accomplish?**

  Specify what you will propose to a particular research field. Be clear and brief while defining the research problem.

- **Why do you want to conduct the research work?**

  Before you begin, ask yourself, why are you doing it? This sounds like an ordinary question but matters the most in research proposals.

It will direct you to conduct a thorough review of the literature. Also, offer convincing evidence to explain the contribution of the topic to the existing field.

- **How will you accomplish it?**

Describe what methods and techniques you will use to conduct the research work. Similarly, also discuss why you are the correct person to carry out this research. However, never make the mistake of proposing a solution that is not feasible.

Here is a detailed guide that will help you write a research paper.

RESEARCH PROPOSAL FORMAT

The research paper steps included in the format are discussed below in detail.

Title Page

A title page is the first section of a research proposal that includes:

- The main title of the research work.
- Student's name.
- Supervisor's name.
- The institution and department.

Abstract and Table of Contents

A research proposal abstract provides a concise summary of your paper in not more than 250 words. On the other hand, an organized table of contents will help the readers to navigate the document. Both these sections are required if the proposal is too long.

Outline

A well-structured research proposal outline is used to organize ideas in a single place. Similarly, it also decides the future headings and subheadings of a research paper.

Research Paper Introduction

The introduction should be brief and catchy to grab the reader's attention. It must include the below-given elements.

- Introduction of the topic.
- Discussion of the main research problem.
- Background of the issue.
- The methodology used to analyze the research problem.
- Significance and importance of the research.
- Future plan for the research.

Background and Significance

The background and significance section explains the detailed context of your research work. You can merge this section with the introduction. However, create a separate section with extensive information if the proposal is lengthy.

Highlight the following key points while writing a background and significance section.

- State the problem and offer a detailed explanation.
- Mention the rationale of the study and indicate why it is worth pursuing.
- Pinpoint the critical issues addressed by the research.
- Explain your chosen type of research methodology and sources that you are planning to use.
- Define the boundaries of the research clearly.
- Write definitions of key terms or concepts for easy understanding.

Literature Review

A comprehensive literature review instills energy in the paper and offers you important insights. It requires a thorough analysis of a literature source that is relevant to the research topic.

Moreover, this section is usually challenging to complete because it contains lots of information. However, a strong literature review aims to convince readers about a valuable contribution to the existing knowledge.

Analyze what research questions are raised by others. Similarly, identify the methods used by them.

Don't be afraid to challenge the findings of others. Nevertheless, make sure that you have challenged their results with substantial and relevant information.

Here are the 5 C's that can make up a literature review.

1. Cite
2. Contrast
3. Compare
4. Connect
5. Critique

By using them, compare and contrast the main theories and methods. Also, identify the strengths and weaknesses of the different approaches while writing a literature review.

Lastly, emphasize how your work will challenge the work of others.

RESEARCH DESIGN AND METHODS

The methodology section explains the overall strategy and steps you should take to address your research questions.

Don't just compose a list of methods. Instead, try to prove that your method is the most relevant and practical approach to answering the questions.

Similarly, always be specific. Choosing multiple methodologies creates confusion in the reader's mind.

The below table will help you identify the methodology in a research proposal.

Research Type	• Qualitative or quantitative research? • Primary or secondary sources? • Research design (descriptive, correlational, and experimental)?
Sources	• How will you select your sources? (case studies, random sampling, etc) • Where will you collect the data? • When will you collect it?
Research	• What tools and

Methods	procedures will be used to collect and analyze the information? (surveys, observations, interviews, experiments)
Practicalities	<ul><li>What is the time required to collect the data?</li><li>How to access participants and sources?</li><li>Are there any challenges and obstacles? How will you deal with them?</li></ul>

Hypothesis

The hypothesis section sets a clear objective for the thesis. It further highlights the implications of the study as per the researcher's view. Moreover, if the hypothesis is clear and understandable, it becomes easy to conduct the research work.

When drafting a potential hypothesis of your thesis, keep in mind the following questions.

- What is going to be the result of your study concerning the theoretical framework and underlying assumptions?
- What possible suggestions could arise from the research outcomes?

- How results will contribute to the natural setting of the workplace?
- Will the outcomes contribute to social and economic problems?
- How outcomes will influence policy decisions?
- How can research work benefit individuals or groups?
- What can be improved as a result of your study?
- How will the outcomes of the study be implemented in the future?

Discussion

The substantive, methodological, and theoretical frameworks are generally highlighted in the discussion. The primary purpose is to analyze the significance of your findings in light of the research problem. Similarly, this section also explores new and fresh insights for future research studies.

It is likely to be connected to the introduction, research questions, and hypothesis. Thus, stick to the purpose of the research to make it easier for the audience to understand.

RESEARCH PAPER CONCLUSION

The conclusion is a summary of the entire research study. It describes the importance and significance of your proposal.

Moreover, this section should be one to two paragraphs long that emphasizes on:

- Why should you conduct the research study?
- How will it advance the existing knowledge?
- How will it benefit other scholars?

Lastly, discuss the prospects for future implications.

Citations

A research proposal formatting must include proper citations for every source that you have used. Similarly, the referencing list should also contain full publication details.

A standard paper proposal has two kinds of citations.

- **References** - Only list the sources you have used in the proposal.
- **Bibliography** - List sources used along with other additional citations that you have studied to conduct the research.

Also, choose the specific citation formats required by the professors. It includes APA, MLA, and Chicago.

Writing the work cited list properly will increase the credibility of your work.

RESEARCH PROPOSAL TOPICS

Below is a list of interesting and easy research proposal topics.

- How can a political system influence society?
- Discuss the difference between Fascism and Nazism.
- How can terrorism affect the economy of a state?
- What is the importance of advertising in running a business?
- Advantages and disadvantages of a testing system.
- Education is the basis for developing a child's character.
- Role of methodology in a research paper.
- Impact of non-governmental organizations.
- How can waste management programs influence society?
- Educational technologies for higher education.

If you still need more ideas, here are some research paper topics to help you choose a good topic.

(back to top)

Research Proposal Writing Strategies

To write a perfect research proposal, follow the below given writing strategies:

- A research proposal should be focused with a clear sense of purpose.

- Landmark works must be cited in the literature review.
- The proposal should also lay a foundation for understanding the scope of the research study.
- It should limit the boundaries of your research (e.g., time, place, or people).
- It must inform the readers how and when the study will examine the main research problem.
- A coherent and persuasive argument should be developed for the research proposal.
- Avoid poor grammar and informal proposal writing. Instead, it must be well-written and follow the rules of good academic writing.
- The proposal should provide enough details about the major issues to support the argument.
- Minor points can also be discussed but should not dominate the overall narrative.

The above guide will help you understand the structure of a research proposal. However, not everyone can write a perfect one. Therefore, most students seek writing help from paper writing services.

Because of having fewer resources, students fall victim to the low-quality research proposals delivered by such scams.

However, some companies offer top quality and original paper at cheap prices. It is because when they claim cheap papers, they refer to the prices and not to the quality.

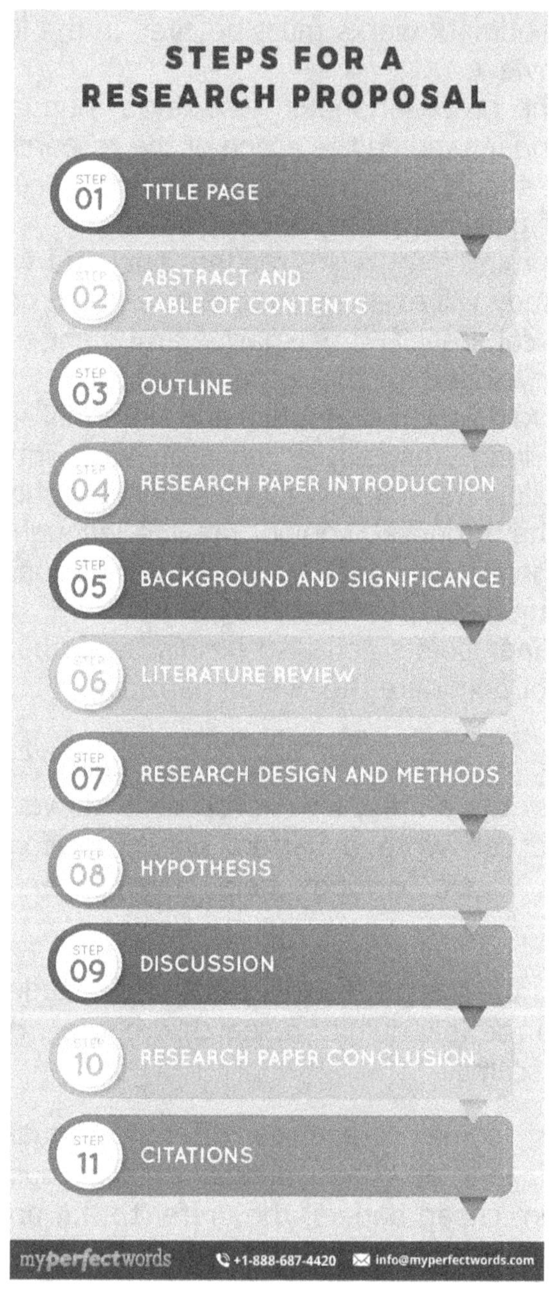

STEPS FOR A
RESEARCH PROPOSAL
STEP 01 TITLE PAGE
STEP 02 ABSTRACT AND TABLE OF CONTENTS
STEP 03 OUTLINE
STEP 04 RESEARCH PAPER INTRODUCTION
STEP 05 BACKGROUND AND SIGNIFICANCE
STEP 06 LITERATURE REVIEW
STEP 07 RESEARCH DESIGN AND METHODS
STEP 08 HYPOTHESIS
STEP 09 DISCUSSION
STEP 10 RESEARCH PAPER CONCLUSION
STEP 11 CITATIONS
myperfectwords
+1-888-687-4420
info@myperfectwords.com

14

WHAT IS HYPOTHESIS?

A hypothesis is a prediction that is more than just a simple guess. Usually, the hypothesis starts with a question that is explored through in-depth research. At this point, you need to develop a strong and testable hypothesis. Your hypothesis should explain what you expect to happen next, except if you are writing an explanatory study.

For example, if exploring the effects of a particular drug, the hypothesis should be what effects this drug might have on the symptoms of a particular disease.

In conducting psychology research, the hypothesis might be how an environment influences a particular response or behavior.

A hypothesis does not have to be accurate always. While it predicts what the researchers expect, the research aims to determine whether the guess came out right or wrong.

A hypothesis also establishes a relationship between two or more variables. A dependable variable is what you observe and measure. An independent variable is what you change or control over time.

DIFFERENT TYPES OF HYPOTHESES

Before heading towards the writing steps, understand the common types of hypotheses with examples.

Simple Hypothesis

A simple hypothesis predicts the connection between the dependent and independent variables. Here are some simple hypothesis examples that you can refer to for your better understanding.

Intake of sugary drinks leads to weight gain.S moking is the leading cause of lung cancer.

Complex Hypothesis

A complex hypothesis predicts the relationship between two or more dependent and two or more independent variables. Follow the below-mentioned complex hypothesis examples and understand how a complex hypothesis is formulated.

Overweight people who value and seek happiness are more likely to lose weight and enjoy life than those who do not care much.Individuals who eat fewer vegetables and more greasy food are at a greater risk of developing heart diseases.

Empirical Hypothesis

An empirical hypothesis is also known as a 'Working hypothesis.' This hypothesis plays a part when the theory is being tested through an experiment and observation. It is no longer just a wild guess. Here are some examples to quickly understand how to craft an empirical hypothesis.

Women who take vitamin E grow their hair faster than those women who take vitamin K.Animals learn faster if the food is given immediately after the response of a command.

Null Hypothesis

A null hypothesis is written when there is not enough information to state the hypothesis or no obvious relationship between the two variables. Refer to the following null hypothesis examples and learn how to disapprove of something.

There is no improvement in my health no matter how healthy I eat or get plenty of sleep.There is no change in my work habits, whether I get 6 hours or 10 hours of sleep.

Alternative Hypothesis

There is always an alternative hypothesis that disapproves of a null hypothesis. It is denoted by H1. You can learn more about the alternative hypothesis with these examples.

My health gets better when I drink green tea daily.My work habits get better when I sleep on time and wake up early in the morning.

Logical Hypothesis

The proposed explanation to process the evidence is a logical hypothesis. Usually, a logical hypothesis is turned into an empirical hypothesis. It aims to put your theories to the test.

Here are some logical hypothesis examples for your better understanding.

Cacti experience more successful growth rates than tulips on Mars.The atmosphere pressure on Mars is less than one-hundredth of what we breathe on Earth.

Statistical Hypothesis

A statistical hypothesis is an examination of a sample of a population. This is the type of analysis in which you use statistical information collected from and for a specific area.

Below are some statistical hypothesis examples to understand how to conduct your research using statistical information.

About 16% of the American population is 65 years old or over.21% of the adults in the United States fall into the category of illiteracy.

HOW TO WRITE A HYPOTHESIS?

Here are the steps that you need to follow for writing a strong hypothesis.

Ask a Question

A hypothesis starts with a research question that you need to address. A clear, focused, and researchable question is required that should be within the limitation of the project.

Conduct Some Initial Research

Now you have to collect data and think about the start of your answer. It should be about the information already known about the research paper topics. Take time and review theories and previous studies to formulate better assumptions.

You can create a conceptual framework to identify which variables you will be focusing on. Also, figure out the relationship between those variables.

Create Your Hypothesis

With the help of theories and previous studies, you might have an idea of what you expect to find. Make sure you come up with a clear and concise initial answer.

Refine Your Hypothesis

Make sure your hypothesis is to the point and testable. Similarly, it can be refined in a variety of ways. All the terms that you use must be defined clearly and contain the following elements.

The required variablesThe group that is being studiedThe predicted outcome of the analysis

Compose Your Hypothesis in Three Different Ways

You can formulate a simple prediction in the form of if...then to identify the variables. The beginning of the sentence should state the independent variable and dependent variable at the end of the sentence.

In academic research, a hypothesis is commonly phrased in terms of defining relations or showing effects. Here you need to state the relationship between variables.

If you are making a comparison, your hypothesis should state what difference you expect.

Formulate a Null Hypothesis

If your research methods cover statistical hypothesis testing, you will need to formulate a null hypothesis. It is donated by 'HO.' A null hypothesis is the default position that shows no connection between the variables.

HYPOTHESIS WRITING TIPS

Here are some of the expert tips that you should keep in mind for writing a good hypothesis.

Do not choose a random topic. Take time and find something interesting to write onKeep the hypothesis to the point, clear, and conciseMake sure to research as it will help you throughout the writing processClearly define your independent and dependent variables

A hypothesis is basically a statement of what you will do. Once you are done writing your hypothesis, you need to test it and analyze the data to come up with your conclusion.

Always refer to the above guide for writing a string hypothesis. However, if you are still not sure, then we at MyPerfectWords.com can provide you with the best help.

We have an expert team of writers who can help you with any type of academic paper and for any academic level. Research papers, case studies, thesis, or any other paper, you can count on us. Simply place your order and get the best writing help at the most affordable rates.

15

HOW TO WRITE AN ABSTRACT

Abstracts have played a critical role in describing the research study to journal editors and researchers. It also encourages them to continue reading the entire research paper.

However, writing a convincing abstract is much more important today than it was before. Thus, it is essential to spend enough time and energy in crafting an abstract that presents the central arguments of your paper.

Similarly, it must also include the key information e.g., summary, results, observations, and trends. Such elements will allow the audience to examine your work easily.

Read this easy guide to master the art of how to write an abstract. Also, learn to come up with unique ideas for captivating readers.

WHAT IS AN ABSTRACT?

It is a well-defined and short summary of longer research work. Moreover, an abstract serves the purpose of informing the readers about the central theme and points of your research. It also describes the aims and outcomes that tell the audience what the full paper is about.

A strong abstract further allows the reader to decide whether he wants to continue with your paper or not. It is an essential part of a research paper and a thesis, and no paper is considered complete without it.

It is about 150 to 250 words long and must be written after completing the paper. Moreover, an abstract comes after the title page and acknowledgments but before the table of content.

TYPES OF AN ABSTRACT

There are four main types of an abstract given below:

- **Critical Abstract -** This type of abstract allows the reader to critically evaluate the paper for analyzing its reliability. It is about 400-500 words in length.
- **Descriptive Abstract -** It usually states the type of information found in the research work in less than 100 words.
- **Informative Abstract -** Like the descriptive abstract, it also mentions the information along with the results, conclusion, and recommendation. The length of the abstract is no more than 300 words.
- **Highlight Abstract -** It is written to provide the complete picture of the research study to attract the readers.

HOW TO WRITE AN ABSTRACT?

Professors usually require students to include an abstract in the research paper. However, this section is often overlooked by the students. Thus, papers with weak abstracts are likely to be rejected by the reviewers.

To write a good abstract, follow the important steps given below.

Check Out the Instructions

Every research paper comes with a set of instructions. These instructions serve as guidelines that every student must follow when writing an abstract. Therefore, before starting a research paper, check out the instructions mentioned by your teacher.

These guidelines may include:

- The type of abstract that you need to write
- A proper structure or pattern that should be followed
- Any specific organization rules to apply
- The required word count
- Style and formatting requirements

Following these instructions will engage the readers to move forward with your paper.

Write the Research Paper First

It is better to write the abstract at the end and after completing the rest of your paper. It is because this section aims to present the important points of your work briefly. Thus, you cannot expect to know them before completing the paper.

Thus, write the research paper before moving to a detail-oriented and good abstract.

Add the Background of the Research Study

Add some background information of your research topic into the abstract. However, avoid adding irrelevant information and lengthy details. Instead, keep the information brief, concise, and focused on the main research question and topic.

Moreover, only choose the facts that are related to your study. It will help you explain the significance of the expected outcome of your research.

Describe the Research Problem and Objectives

Start your abstract by clearly describing the purpose and objectives of your research. Explain its significance to the people, society, and a field of study. Also, discuss which research question(s) do you aim to answer in your paper.

For this, use words such as evaluate, analyze, and investigate. Moreover, this section can be written in simple past or present tense but can never be in the future.

Similarly, to state your research problem, answer the following questions:

- Why are you conducting this research?
- How will the study contribute to the field?
- Why should the audience read the entire paper?
- What is the main problem that your research is trying to solve?
- What is the scope of the study i.e., specific or general?
- What is the major argument?

Mention the Research Methods

Every research work follows a specific methodology. Here, mention the research methods that you have used to answer the research question.

It consists of 1 to 2 sentences that are usually written in the past tense. Do not try to explain everything in it. Rather, be concise and brief.

The main goal here is to give an overall idea of the approaches, procedures, and sources that you have used. It can be qualitative, quantitative, case study, etc. Simply state your reasons for choosing a particular method and why it benefits your research.

Discuss the Previous Researches

Some abstracts discuss the relevant and previous researches on the chosen topic. However, after identifying them, you must also mention a unique perspective you are working on.

Make sure it should not be too detailed and lengthy. Instead, just provide a brief overview to indicate that your research study is different from others.

An abstract is considered as a mini version of the research. Thus, add enough information to keep the reader engaged. Nevertheless, ensure that you mention the key points only if the explanation comes later in the body of your paper.

Summarize Findings and Results

Summarize the major findings and results of your study in this section. Write in simple past and present tense and avoid using vague qualitative terms.

Also, identify the contribution of your study in concrete terms i.e., percentage, trends, figures, etc. Similarly, also compare the methods and results with the hypothesis by stating whether the study was successful or not.

State Your Conclusion

State the conclusion of your research in the last section of the abstract. It must explain the answer to your research question and problem.

Also, mention research limitations briefly, if there are any. It can be related to the sample size or the methodology. It will enable the audience to understand the credibility of the research work and the circumstances in which it has been carried out.

Similarly, a writer can also make suggestions and recommendations for future research and a call to action in this section. Make sure your results add value to the respective field of knowledge.

Use Keywords to Attract the Audience

Add a list of keywords at the end of your abstract to attract the audience. These should be the most common and relevant terms.

By referencing such keywords with your research, the potential readers can find your paper easily during their searches. Thus, include 5 to 10 short words that are central to your research study.

Remember, the Publication Manuals of the American Psychological (APA) style has some specific requirements for formatting these keywords.

Read Some Abstract Samples

Learning through examples is the best and fastest way of learning anything. Before writing your paper's abstract, read some online samples related to different subjects. These disciplines may include science, social sciences, and humanities.

Reading samples while writing a literature review gives a good idea of the type of abstract that each subject should have.

Make a Rough Draft First

Make a rough draft of your abstract. At this stage, do not think of the word limit or the type of content you are using. Just focus on the main theme of your paper and write down everything that crosses your mind.

However, avoid adding the following elements in the abstract.

- Lengthy background details
- Unnecessary phrases, adverbs, and adjectives
- Repetitive information
- Acronyms or abbreviations
- References to other research work
- Incomplete sentences
- Ellipticals or jargon language
- Citations to others work
- Any type of image, table, or illustration
- Definitions of the keywords and terms

After writing, review and revise it thoroughly. Remove everything that gives away too much of details. Make sure it is concise and just give a hint of the information included in the main sections.

Proofread Before Submission

No writing process is complete without the final and detailed proofreading. Once you are done writing the abstract, proofread and edit it carefully.

Many students try to avoid this part and submit the paper without proper proofreading. As a result, they end up with low grades.

Also, read the rest of the paper and double-check the results section before you hand it over to your teacher. Refer to the below-given document to get a detailed idea of writing an abstract for a research paper.

TIPS TO WRITE AN ABSTRACT FOR A RESEARCH PAPER

To write an effective abstract for a paper, follow the useful tips given below.

- Write the abstract by using a reverse outlining process. Make a list of keywords for each section. Draft a few sentences that summarize the central argument. Revise them to get a clear framework of your research abstract.
- Read other sample abstracts to get a better idea of the style and structure.
- Write clearly and concisely by avoiding unnecessary words and jargon language. Make sure that each sentence should present one major argument. It will make it easy for readers to understand the topic.
- Present the original contributions of your research instead of discussing other's work.

Writing an abstract for a paper is not as hard as you think. It requires proper structure and detail. But, it is definitely something that you can achieve with practice and hard work. Following this above-given step by step guide will help you write a perfect abstract of your research paper.

However, not every student has the talent and skills to come up with a strong abstract. Therefore, they end up taking help from an online paper writing service for complete guidance.

16

HOW TO WRITE A LITERATURE REVIEW

A literature review requires a lot of research work. Most students contemplate it as the hardest and complicated part while writing a research paper. Besides, you may also have to write it as a stand-alone assignment.

Drafting a strong literature review is considered as the foundation of any research. It helps to evaluate existing research and tells your teacher how your research is relevant to the respective field. Moreover, it also discusses new insights that your research will contribute to the field of study.

Thus, a writer needs to be well prepared to utilize multiple scholarly sources to find the required research material. An organizational plan must also be developed to combine both the summary and synthesis of the previous literature.

Keep on reading this complete guide to learning how to write a literature review paper in simple steps.

What is a Literature Review?

A literature review is the research and evaluation of the available literature in your chosen topic area. It includes a survey of scholarly sources to provide an overview of the current research and available data and knowledge.

These sources include books, journal articles, and newspapers, that relate to your research question.

Moreover, it not only summarizes the sources. But it also analyzes, interprets, and evaluates the relevant theories, methods, points of view, and gaps in the existing literature.

However, this does not mean that a literature review is based on previous searches only. The writer discusses the research question and its various aspects and discusses the relevant study to support this claim.

What is the Importance of a Good Literature Review?

Some of the key reasons to add a literature review into your research paper, thesis, and dissertation include:

- It shows that the writer is familiar with the topic and the relevant literature.
- It helps to develop a theoretical framework and methodology for your research.
- It positions a writer in relation to other researchers and scholars.
- It enables you to identify a research gap and contribute to filling that void by contributing to the field.
- It resolves any conflicts between the previous studies.

The length of a literature review usually depends on the length of the research project. For example, if you are writing a research paper of 10 pages. You will have to include 5 to 6 sources in your literature review.

However, consulting with the professor about proper requirements beforehand is a better way to avoid any last-minute issues.

HOW TO WRITE A LITERATURE REVIEW?

To write a good literature review for a research paper, follow the given steps.

Search Relevant Literature

The first important step before starting a review section is to have a clearly defined topic.

Writing a literature review for a research paper requires you to search for literature. It should be relevant to your research problem and questions. Similarly, use the keywords to search for different sources.

To find the relevant journals and articles, look for the following useful academic databases.

- The institution's library catalog
- Google Scholar
- EBSCO
- JSTOR

However, for writing a review as a stand-alone assignment, develop a research question that gives direction to your search.

Such a question must be answered without gathering original data. Instead, you should answer it by reviewing the existing material.

Furthermore, create a list of keywords related to the topic and research question. Find useful articles and check for the reference list to come up with more authentic sources.

You probably would not be able to cover everything on the chosen topic. Thus, begin by reading the abstract to identify whether the article is relevant or not.

Also, take enough time to evaluate the sources. Make a list of citations and ensure there are no repetitive authors, articles, or publications in the literature review.

Analyze and Select Sources

Obviously, it is impossible to read each and every single thing written about the research topic. Instead, you have to analyze the sources that are most relevant to your research questions.

Answer the below questions while analyzing each source.

- What is the question or problem that the writer has been discussing?

- How the key concepts are defined?
- What theories, approaches, and methods are addressed?
- Does the research study follow an established or innovative approach?
- What are the key findings of the research work?
- How is the literature related to other publications?
- Does the study pose any challenges to the existing literature?
- What are the possible contributions to the field knowledge?
- Discuss the key arguments.
- Elaborate on the strengths and weaknesses of the research work.

Make sure you are using credible and authentic sources. Also, read the important publications and articles to justify your argument.

Moreover, the scope of the literature review largely depends on the topic and discipline. For example, science students only evaluate recent literary work to write their reviews. Nevertheless, the humanities students also have to study and discuss the historical research and perspective about the topic.

Begin the writing process along with searching and reading the relevant sources. Note down important information to use in the text of your literature review.

It is better to cite your sources at this stage to avoid the risk of plagiarism. Moreover, it can also help in developing an annotated bibliography.

Identify Connections

Start organizing the argument and structure of a literature review. For this, you have to identify the connection between the sources that are used while writing an abstract.

Based on your evaluation, you can look for the following things:

- **Trends or Patterns:** What theories and methods can become more or less popular over time?
- **Themes:** What concepts repeatedly occur?
- **Debate and Conflicts:** What conflicts do the source have?
- **Gaps:** What is missing in the literature and what elements further need to be addressed?
- **Influential Literature:** Are there any influential research work available that can change the direction of the field?

These elements will help you identify your contribution to the existing knowledge.

Decide the Structure

There are various approaches that can be used to organize the literature review. Depending upon the length, it can follow a chronological, thematic, methodological, or theoretical framework.

The approaches to organizing a review are discussed below in detail.

- **Chronological**

  It is the simplest approach to structure your literature review. However, do not just summarize and list the sources. Instead, analyze the critical debates, research, and patterns that have shaped the direction of the field. Also, discuss your interpretation of the developments.

- **Thematic**

  This type of approach helps to organize the review into subsections. Each section will discuss a different aspect of the chosen topic.

- **Methodological**

  It helps to compare the outcomes of gathering sources from different research methods. It may include the analysis of:

    - Results emerged from a qualitative vs quantitative approach.
    - Discussion of the topic through an empirical and theoretical approach.

o   Division of the literature into historical, and cultural sources.

- **Theoretical**

  A literature review is often used to discuss various theories and key concepts. By using this approach, you can argue the relevance of a particular theoretical method. Similarly, you can also combine different theories to make a new framework for your research.

WRITE YOUR LITERATURE REVIEW

Like any other academic paper, a literature review format must have three sections: introduction, body section, and a conclusion. What to include in each section depends on the aims and objectives of your literature review.

Literature Review Introduction

It is the first paragraph that clearly defines the purpose and focus of the review.

If your literature review is part of your thesis or dissertation, restate the research question. Similarly, briefly summarize the whole context by highlighting literature gaps.

If you are writing a standalone literature review, provide background information on the topic. Also, discuss the scope of the literature and your research objectives. However, don't forget to mention the results that you will draw from the literature.

Literature Review Body

Divide the body into subsections for each theme or a methodological approach. While writing the body of a literature review, keep in mind the following things.

- Provide an overview of the key points of each source and combine them coherently.
- Do not just paraphrase other's research, make your own interpretations where possible.
- Discuss the significance of your findings in relation to your research.
- State the strengths and weaknesses of the sources.
- Make use of the transitions and topic sentences to write well-structured body paragraphs.

Literature Review Conclusion

Summarize your key findings and emphasize their significance in the conclusion section.

While writing a conclusion for a dissertation or thesis, demonstrate the research gaps and your contributions. Also, discuss how you have developed the research framework by using the theories and methods.

However, a conclusion of a stand-alone literature review will discuss the overall implications and suggestions for future research.

Edit and Proofread

Once you are done with the writing process, don't forget to edit and proofread your paper. It will help you ensure that the paper does not miss anything important and is free from grammatical, and spelling mistakes.

Have a look at the below-given document to learn writing a literature review.

COMMON MISTAKES TO AVOID

The following are some common mistakes that should be avoided while writing a perfect literature review.

- Students do not take sufficient time to define and identify the most relevant sources.
- Sources of your literature review are not related to the research problem.
- Excessive reliance on secondary sources rather than relevant primary data.
- Accepting other research findings as valid rather than critically examining the research design and analysis.
- Not describing the search procedures to identify the review of the literature.

- Only considering statistical results as valid rather than integrating the chi-squared or meta-analytic methods.
- Not considering the research findings and interpretations found in the literature.

There is a considerable amount of effort that goes into the literature review writing process. It is a complicated academic assignment that you get at high school, college, or university.

Some students lack good writing skills and for some, it is just a boring task. Thus, they look for professional help to deal with such a complex assignment.

This detailed guide will help you learn how to do a literature review in no time. However, you can take help from an essay writing company that can help you write perfect literature reviews for research papers.

17

HOW TO CITE A RESEARCH PAPER

Citation is an important part of all academic work, including essays, research papers, theses, and dissertations, and without them, the students could land in dire trouble. There is no single way of citing an academic work, and, usually, the teacher specifies the citation style when assigning the work.

Different citation styles and referencing styles follow different formats, and the students have to follow the format closely and properly when working on any style. However, not all of those styles are simple, and some are quite difficult to follow.

This blog explains different kinds of citation styles and ways of citing in each of them.

Stay with us and read on to know more.

What is a Citation Style?

A citation style is a set of rules and guidelines that help the students format their papers in a certain way. It is important when referring to other people's work and using the details and sources of other researchers.

Usually, the citation styles are published in official handbooks and booklets, and they also have relevant and ample examples, instructions, and explanations to help the readers understand better.

The information added in all of the citation styles remains the same. It includes the author's full name, the name of the cited work, the year of publication, page numbers, the name of the website, and the place of publication. However, the order in which they are presented is different in every citation style.

When working on any of the styles, it is important to follow these details and format them accordingly.

Why is Following Citation Styles Important?

The main reason to cite the added sources and details is to avoid academic theft and intellectual dishonesty. Adding and presenting ideas and quotes of other scholars and researchers without crediting them properly is punishable by law. The person would even have to face legal consequences.

It is also important because, with them, you credit and recognize the right people. Below are some core reasons to add citations to your work.

- **To avoid plagiarism and credit the actual writers and researchers** - It is important because you should acknowledge the actual writers and respect their efforts.

- **To conform to intellectual property rights** - When conducting the research, sometimes you may come across information and details that are intellectually protected.

Some of such details include patented material, trademarks, industrial designs, creative works, and architectural designs. If you use any of such things without crediting them, then they could complain about you.

- **To add and provide proof of your research** - Citing the added details, studies, and research proves the credibility of your work.
- **Helps the readers check the presented data themselves** - With proper text citation and references, the readers could check the facts and original sources themselves. This shows your credibility and honesty also.

Adding citations to research work is important as they help save you from intellectual theft and maintain a good stance as a researcher.

How to Cite a Research Paper in Different Referencing Styles?

As mentioned earlier, different referring styles follow different patterns in which the details are added and presented. Below, we have explained some of the important citation styles and ways to cite them correctly.

APA Research Paper Format

The American Psychological Association, APA is probably the most commonly used citation style. An

APA style is more common in some subjects of humanities, psychology, and social sciences.

It is also the simplest kind of citation, and students and researchers use it to format their work.

General Guidelines - The paper should be double-spaced, have 1" margins on all sides and written in the Times New Roman font style. Other than this, you can use any other font style that is easy to read and understand.

Add a header on top of each page. The header must have a short title of your essay's name and the page number in the top right corner.

Below are the different citation formats for different kinds of sources.

- **For Books:** Author, A.A.. (Year of Publication). The Title of work. Publisher City, State: Publisher.

  Example: Williams, J. (1970). Time and Again. New York, NY: Simon and Schuster.

- **For Magazines:** Author, A.A.. (Year, a month of Publication). Article title. Magazine Title, Volume(Issue), pp.-pp.

  Example: Tumulty, K. (2006, April). Should they stay, or should they go? Time, 167(15), 3-40.

- **For Newspapers:** Author, A.A.. (Year, Month Date of Publication). Article title. Magazine Title, pp. xx-xx.

Example: Rosenberg, G. (1997, March 31). Electronic discovery proves an effective legal weapon. The New York Times, p. D5.

- **For Websites:** Author, A.A.. (Year, Month Date of Publication). Article title. Retrieved from URL

    Example: Simmons, B. (2015, January 9). The tale of two Flaccos. Retrieved from {link}

For multiple authors, you do not have to add all the authors in the list or even in the in-text citation. For more, read a complete APA format guide and learn to style your paper and citations accordingly.

MLA Research Paper Format

MLA or the Modern Language Association is another common citation style, second to APA only, and is usually used in the field and subjects of humanities and liberal arts. This citation helps the writers and researchers add detailed and more refined information in the essays and other academic work.

General Guidelines - This kind of essay or research paper does not have a separate title page, and the details are added on the first page of the essay. The page is double-spaced and with 1" margins on all four sides of the page. The preferred font size is 12 pt. and Times New Roman is generally used.

The heading added on the first page to the upper left corner of the page must include the following details;

- Your full name
- The full name of your teacher
- Course title
- Date of submission

The upper right corner of the header will include your last name and the page number.

Here is the MLA style citation to cite sources of different kinds.

- **For Books:** Last Name, First Name. Book Title. Publisher City: Publisher Name, Year Published. Medium.

  Example: Smith, John. The Sample Book. Pittsburgh: BibMe, 2008. Print.

- **For Magazines:** Last Name, First Name. "Article Title." Magazine Name Publication Date: Page Numbers. Medium.

  Example: Smith, John. "Obama inaugurated as President." Time 21 Jan. 2009: 21-23. Print.

- **For Newspapers:** Last Name, First Name. "Article Title." Newspaper Name Publication Date: Page Numbers. Medium.

  Example: Smith, John. "Steelers win Super Bowl XLIII." Pittsburgh Post-Gazette 2 Feb. 2009: 4-6. Print.

- **For Websites:** Last Name, First Name. "Page Title." Website Title. Sponsoring Institution/Publisher. Publication Date: Page Numbers. Medium.

Example: Smith, John. "Obama inaugurated as President." CNN.com. Cable News Network, 21 Jan. 2009. Web. 1 Feb. 2009.

A comprehensive MLA format guide will help you know and understand this style guide properly. The style uses parenthetical citations and refers to its references as 'Works Cited.'

Chicago Style Research Paper Format

Chicago style is a common citation style that is used in the girls of humanities. It is different from both the APA and MLA citation styles, and besides citing references, the student has to add additional information and details in the endnotes and footnotes sections. The style allows the students to add credible literature and references to the content.

General Guidelines - The paper should have 1" margins on all four sides of the page, must be double-spaced, and written in Times New Roman font. However, the double-space will not apply to table titles, blockquotes, captions of the figures, and due dates.

The page numbers will be added in the header of the first page and will begin with number 1. The page numbering will continue throughout the entire paper, including the reference list and bibliography.

Here is how you should cite different sources in a Chicago style paper.

- **For Books:** Last Name, First Name. Title of Book. Publisher City: Publisher Name, Year Published.

  Example: Brown, Dan. The DaVinci Code. New York: Scholastic, 2004.

- **For Magazines:** Last Name, First Name. Article title. Magazine Title, Month Date, Year of publication.

  Example: Chan, Dan. The art of pandas. Panda Magazine, Nov 10, 1985.

- **For Newspapers:** Last Name, First Name. "Article Title." Newspaper Name, Publication Date.

  Example: Smith, John. "Steelers win Super Bowl XLIII." Pittsburgh Post-Gazette, February 2, 2009.

- **For Websites:** Last Name, First Name. "Page Title." Website Title. Web Address (retrieved Date Accessed).

  Example: Smith, John. "Obama inaugurated as President." {link} (accessed February 1, 2009).

Chicago style format has many other conventions also, and you can learn them by going through a detailed guide.

ASA Research Paper Format

The citation style is developed by the Sociological Association. The students, researchers, and scholars of Sociology use this citation style for writing their university research papers.

These papers are related to Sociology, and the style is also used for submitting research articles to peer-reviewed ASA journals.

General Guidelines - The paper must have a separate abstract page before the title page, and the title must be added again as a heading. The abstract should not exceed 200 words and should be precise and brief.

The preferred font style and size are Times New Roman and 12 pt. with 1 to ¼ inches of margins on all sides of the page.

The page numbers should be added on every page and in the top right corner. ASA style research papers must also have three to five keywords that the writer should mention at the beginning of the paper.

Here is how you should cite different kinds of sources in an ASA paper.

- **For Books:** Author's Last and First Name. Year of Publication. Title. Country of Publisher: Publisher.

  Example: James, Henry. 2003. The Turn of the Screw. New York: Barnes & Noble Books.

- **For E-Books:** Author's Last and First Name. Year of Publication. Title. Country of Publisher: Publisher. Retrieved Month Day, Year {link}.

  Example: James, Henry. 2003. The Turn of the Screw. New York: Penguin Books Kindle Version. Retrieved January 18, 2017. {link}

- **For Journal Articles:** Author's Last and First Name. Year of Publication. "Title." Journal Name issue #: inclusive page numbers.

  Example: Feekins, Bo. 2008. "Chasing Tree Frogs." National Geographic #182. 6-10

- **For Magazine Articles:** Author's Last and First Name. Year of Pub. "Title." Magazine Name, Month Year, pp. Inclusive page numbers.

  Example: Geary, Rachel. 2012. "The Issue with Mastery Learning." New York Times, April 2002. Pp. 15-23.

- **For Websites:** Author's Last and First Name. Date of Publishing. Title. Publisher. Retrieved Month Day, Year {link}.

  Example: Lee, Bruce. 03.09.2004. Birth of a Nation. Retrieved 18.01.2017. {link}

Read this complete ASA format and citation guide to know more about the citation style.

IEEE Style Research Paper Format

The IEEE style is used in the field and study of electronics, engineering, computer science, and telecommunication. The style is managed by a professional organization for various technical industries and IEEE stands for the Institute for Electrical and Electronics Engineers (IEEE).

The in-text citations used in this format are added in the form of numbered brackets that further refer to full-length references.

General Guidelines - The page layout should be as follows:

- Top - 19mm (0.75")
- Bottom - 43mm (1.69")
- Left & Right - 14.32mm (0.56")

The text font should be Times New Roman and the font size should be 10 pt. The spacing should be single and the first line of each paragraph should be indented.

Here is the citation guide for different sources in the IEEE format.

- **For Books:** J. K. Author, "Title of chapter in the book," in Title of His Published Book, xth ed. City of Publisher, (only U.S. State), Country: Abbrev. of Publisher, year, ch. x, sec. x, pp. xxx–xxx.

  Example: [1] W. K. Chen, Linear Networks and Systems. Belmont, CA: WadsworthPress, 2003.

- **For Conference Papers**: J. K. Author, "Title of paper," presented at the Abbreviated Name of Conf., City of Conf., Abbrev. State, Country, Month and day(s), year, Paper number.

  Example: D. Caratelli, M. C. Viganó, G. Toso, and P. Angeletti, "Analytical placement technique for sparse arrays," presented at the 32nd ESA Antenna Workshop, Noordwijk, The Netherlands, Oct. 5p, 2010.

- **For Periodicals:** J. K. Author, "Name of paper," Abbrev. Title of Periodical, vol. x, no. x, pp. xxx-xxx, Abbrev. Month, year.

  Example: M. Ito et al., "Application of amorphous oxide TFT to electrophoretic display," J. Non-Cryst. Solids, vol. 354, no. 19, pp. 2777–2782, Fp. 2008.

- **For Software Manuals:** J. K. Author (or Abbrev. Name of Co., City of Co. Abbrev. State, Country). Name of Manual/Handbook, x ed. (year). Accessed: Date. [Online]. Available: http://www.url.com

  Example: L. Breimann. Manual on Setting Up, Using, and Understanding Random Forests v4.0. (2003). Accessed: Apr. 16, 2014. [Online]. Available: http://oz.berkeley.edu/users/breiman/Using_random_forests_v4.0.pdfpli>

For more about IEEE style first, read the complete IEEE citation and format guide.

Apart from these, there are many other citation styles that are commonly used in many fields and research work. Some things are common in them, like in all styles, the quotes are added in quotation marks, and they have the same details, just in a different order.

18
TOOLS IN RESEARCH

RESEARCH TOOLS AND TECHNIQUES

Quantitative research tools

Quantitative methods involve the collection and analysis of objective data, often in numerical form. The research design is determined prior to the start of data collection and is not flexible. The research process, interventions and data collection tools (e.g. questionnaires) are standardized to minimize or control possible bias.

Qualitative research techniques and tools

Qualitative research is generally used to explore values, attitudes, opinions, feelings and behaviours of individuals and understand how these affect the individuals in question. Researchers using qualitative methods are concerned with individuals' perceptions of specific topics, issues or situations and the meanings they assign to their lives. This kind of research is important for generating theory, developing policy, improving educational practice, justifying change for a particular practice, and illuminating social issues. It may also be used to explain the results of a previous quantitative study or to prepare for the development of a quantitative study.

If your research team decides to use qualitative methods in your study, you will need to describe how qualitative methods will provide the information to help you address your research objectives and research question(s). For example, qualitative research may be appropriate because you intend to explore the values and behaviours of individuals in the study area in relation to a public health intervention, and to understand how these affect the phenomena in question. For example, why do some households have bed nets but do not use them? Or, why do individuals in a study area decline services from a specialized antenatal clinic? Qualitative methods can provide context, a deeper understanding of stakeholders' needs and participants' perspectives.

When collecting qualitative data, it is preferable to use more than one data collection method. Obtaining information on the same phenomena in a variety of ways allows the researcher to triangulate the data, adding rigour to the research. By nature, qualitative data collection is emergent and the design is intentionally flexible to enable the researcher investigate themes (findings) in more detail as they emerge.

Qualitative methods use data collection methodologies such as interviewing, observation, discussions and review of documents (e.g. diaries, historical documents). The results of qualitative research are descriptive or explanatory rather than predictive, and are typically time-consuming to collect and analyse. The following table may be helpful to you as you decide which qualitative tools and techniques are most appropriate for your IR project.

Unlike quantitative data collection, qualitative data collection can be more flexible allowing the research to incorporate emerging themes in the ongoing data collection. This allows the researcher to test and validate findings as they collect the data. For example, perhaps in one in-depth interview, the researcher learns that people do not attend the lymphatic filariasis mass drug administration because they use traditional medicines and therefore feel that they are already under treatment. The researcher may then add a related question to subsequent in-depth interviews to see how prevalent this phenomenon is in the study population.

Pre-testing

All study instruments (quantitative and qualitative) should be pre-tested to check the validity and reliability of data collection tools. Pre-testing allows the research team to check whether the research instructions and questions are clear, context specific, and that adequate time has been allowed to administer the questionnaire, etc. Pre-testing should be conducted from a comparable study population and environment. Since data management is critical to the success of the research, the data management team should be available during the discussion that follows the pre-test, in order to incorporate changes into the final design of the tool and facilitate the incorporation of appropriate checks into the data entry system. This stage includes designing the forms for recording measurements, developing programmes for data entry, management and analysis; and planning dummy tabulations to ensure the appropriate variables are collected.

SOURCES

Scholarly articles are a great resource for finding *in-depth, current information on a topic*. Scholarly articles have a more narrow focus than books, so you can try searching for more specific topics.

- This type of article may also be called **peer-reviewed articles**, or **refereed articles**.
- Scholarly articles are one of the most common types of sources your professors will require you to include in your research.
- Scholarly articles are found in journals, which you can search for in a **database.**

The McQuade Library subscribes to over 220 databases that range from **general** to **subject-specific.**

What Makes a Book Scholarly?

How can you tell if a book is scholarly?

The fastest way is to check the publisher- if it's published by a university press (e.g. Chicago, Harvard, etc.) or other academic presses (e.g., Blackwell, Routledge, Palgrave, Ashgate) it is scholarly. Another way to decide is to look at the book's intended audience and purpose.

How are scholarly books different from regular books?

Scholarly books are published with the goal of contributing to research and knowledge of a subject, and support future research by scholars and students, not necessarily making money.

Who decides whether or not a scholarly book gets published?

All scholarly books go through an extensive process in which experts in the field read the manuscripts and decide if the book is worthy to be published. In other words, scholarly books are peer reviewed sources.

Remember, scholarly books are just one of many kinds of books available through the library. If you are unsure if the book you have found is scholarly ask a librarian or your professor.

Understanding Primary, Secondary, and Tertiary Sources

Magazine or Journal?

When searching for articles, it's important to know what type of source, or periodical in which the articles are published. This is beacuse each type has its own purpose, intent, audience, etc. This guide lists criteria to help you identify scholarly journals, trade journals, and magazines. It is the first step in critically evaluating your source of information.

Determining what makes a journal scholarly is not a clear-cut process, but there are many indicators which can help you.

Scholarly Journal

- Reports original research or experimentation
- Articles written by an expert in the field for other experts in the field
- Articles use specialized jargon of the discipline
- Articles undergo peer review process before acceptance for publication in order to assure creative content
- Authors of articles always cite their sources in the form of footnotes or bibliographies

Examples:

Journal of Asian Studies

Psychophysiology

Social Research

A note about "peer review." Peer review insures that the research reported in a journal's article is sound and of high quality. Sometimes the term "refereed" is used instead of peer review.

Trade Journal

- Discusses practical information in industry
- Contains news, product information, advertising, and trade articles
- Contains information on current trends in technology

- Articles usually written by experts in the field for other experts in the field
- Articles use specialized jargon of the discipline
- Useful to people in the trade field and to people seeking orientation to a vocation

Examples:

Advertising Age

Independent Banker

People Management

General Interest Magazines

- Provides information in a general manner to a broad audience
- Articles generally written by a member of the editorial staff or a freelance writer
- Language of articles geared to any educated audience, no subject expertise assumed
- Articles are often heavily illustrated, generally with photographs
- No peer review process
- Sources are sometimes cited, but more often there are no footnotes or bibliography

Examples:

Newsweek

Popular Science

Psychology Today

Popular Magazine

- Articles are short and written in simple language with little depth to the content of these articles
- The purpose is generally to entertain, not necessarily inform
- Information published in popular magazines is often second-or third-hand
- The original source of information contained in articles is obscure
- Articles are written by staff members or freelance writers

Examples:

People

Rolling Stone

Working Woman

How do you find scholarly journals?

The McQuade Library has many online periodical databases which contain scholarly journal articles. Databases such as EBSCOhost and INFOTRAC allow you to limit your search to peer reviewed or refereed journals.

If you have found an article and are not sure if it is scholarly or not you can find out by consulting the following books located in the Reference Room:

LaGuardia, Cheryl, Magazines for Libraries, 12th ed., New Providence, NJ: R.R. Bowker. (Ref Z 6941 .K2 2003)

Ulrich's International Periodicals Directory, New York: Bowker, 2003. (Ref Z 6941 .U5 2003)

If you need assistance or require further information please ask a librarian.

The information contained in this brochure was adapted from Working with Faculty to Design Undergraduate Information Literacy Programs: A How-To-Do-It Manual for Librarians by Rosemary Young, New York: Neal Schuman, 1999. (Updated 01/07/04)

Features of a Peer-Reviewed Article (Loyd Sealy Library)

When you are determining whether or not the article you found is a peer-reviewed article, you should consider the following.

Does the article have the following features?

Been published in a scholarly journal.

An overall **serious, thoughtful tone**.

More than 10 pages in **length** (usually, but not always).

An abstract (summary) on the first page.

Organization by headings such as Introduction, Literature Review, and Conclusion.

Citations throughout and a bibliography or reference list at the end.

Credentialed authors, usually affiliated with a research institute or university.

Ethnic and Racial Studies
Vol. 38, No. 15, 2615–2634, http://dx.doi.org/10.1080/01419870.2015.1077986

Patterns of minority and majority identification in a multicultural society

Alita Nandi and Lucinda Platt

(Received 2 October 2014, accepted 20 April 2015)

There has been increasing investigation of the national and ethnic identification of minority populations in Western societies and how far they raise questions about the success or failure of multicultural societies. Much of the political and academic discussion has, however, been premised on two assumptions. First, that ethnic minority and national identification are mutually exclusive, and, second, that national identification forms an overarching majority identity that represents consensus values. In this paper, using a large-scale nationally representative UK survey with a varied set of identity questions, and drawing on an extension of Berry's acculturation framework, we empirically test these two assumptions. We find that, among minorities, strong British national and minority identities often coincide and are not on an opposing axis. We also find that adherence to a British national identity shows cleavages within the white majority population. We further identify variation in these patterns by generation and political orientation.

Introduction

There has been extensive recent debate on the success or otherwise of 'multiculturalism'. On one side has been the claim that the multiculturalist project can incorporate diverse populations within a common framework (Kymlicka 1996; Modood 2007; Parekh 2000). On the other, there has been an explicit anxiety about the extent to which multicultural responses to diversity foster exclusive minority and religious identities and undermine common cause (Cameron 2011; Huntington 1993). The endorsement of national identity by minorities is often taken to be an indicator of their incorporation into the receiving country society, and to represent both acceptance of shared national values and implicit rejection of ethnic or cultural distinctiveness (Reeskens and Wright 2013). Conversely, maintenance of strong ethnic identities is read as problematic for an integrated society and a challenge to a national

ALITA NANDI is Research Fellow in the Institute for Social and Economic Research at Essex University. anandi@essex.ac.uk
LUCINDA PLATT is Professor in the Department of Social Policy at the LSE. L.Platt@lse.ac.uk

Also consider...

- Is the journal in which you found the article published or sponsored by a professional scholarly society, professional association, or university academic department? Does it describe itself as a peer-reviewed publication? (To know that, check the journal's website).
- Did you find a citation for it in one of the databases that includes scholarly publications? (Academic Search Complete, PsycINFO, etc.)? Read the database description to see if it includes scholarly publications.
- In the database, did you limit your search to **scholarly** or **peer-reviewed** publications? (See video tutorial below for a demonstration.)
- Is the topic of the article **narrowly focused and explored in depth**?
- Is the article based on either **original research** or **authorities in the field** (as opposed to personal opinion)?
- Is the article written for readers with some prior knowledge of the subject?
- If your field is social or natural science, is the article divided into sections with headings such as those listed below?

<table>
<tr><td>

- Introduction
- Theory Background
- Methods
- Discussion

</td><td>or</td><td>

- Literature review
- Subjects
- Results
- Conclusion

</td></tr>
</table>

List of credible sources for research

According to Gahan (2021), it is crucial that you use credible primary and secondary sources to ensure the validity of your academic research, but knowing which ones are credible can be difficult!

Luckily, there are some tricks for helping you figure out if a source is credible, which we have outlined in our guide to evaluating sources using the CRAAP test.

If you are not sure where to begin, we have collected a list of credible sources to help point you in the right direction.

Credible websites

Many sources you will find online might not be verified or contain accurate information, so it is important that you use the right websites to help your research.

Government and educational websites (.gov or .edu), such as those of universities, are your safest bet for finding accurate information with no hidden agenda. You might be tempted to use and cite Wikipedia, but you need to be very careful with this as it is not considered a proper academic source.

You also need to be careful of native advertising, advertorials and public relations content that might be designed to sell a product rather than provide reliable information. Read more about evaluating website credibility.

RECOMMENDED CREDIBLE RESEARCH WEBSITES

Website	Subject
Science.gov	The US government's official site for all things science. Search more than 60 databases and 2,200 websites, with access to over 200 million authoritative pages.
US Census Bureau	All the latest and historic census data for the United States.
UK Statistics	The UK's Office for National Statistics. Includes data, design and background information on previous censuses conducted in the UK.
US Government	Information on the US government, including laws, historical documents, past Presidents and more.
UK Government	Information on government services, legal processes and major events in the UK.
Smithsonian	The Smithsonian Institute's official online magazine, offering a variety of

Website	Subject
Magazine	articles on history, science, arts and culture, technology and more. The Institute is administered by the US Government.
Encyclopedia Britannica	The online Encyclopedia Britannica. A great place to find information on general topics, including biographies, history, country information, religion and much more.
National Bureau of Economic Research	A non-profit, non-partisan US organization that conducts research on the subject of economy and distributes findings for academics, policy makers and professionals.

CREDIBLE SOURCES FOR JOURNAL ARTICLES

Assessing the credibility of a journal article is easier than with any other source, as many sites include information such as how many times the work has been cited, whether or not it has been peer reviewed (approved by other researchers), and links to background on the author(s).

Whenever you are in doubt, apply the CRAAP Test, considering the currency, relevance, authority, accuracy and purpose of the journal article.

The Journal Quality List provides further assistance with understanding the level of credibility of a particular journal.

RECOMMENDED SOURCES FOR JOURNAL ARTICLES

Subject	Journal source
General	JSTOR
	Google Scholar
	Oxford Academic, part of the Oxford University Press
	Microsoft Academic
	Cornell University Library
	SAGE Publishing
	Taylor and Francis Online
	Academic Journals
	OAIster

Subject	Journal source
	Directory of Open Access Journals
Science	Science Mag
	OMICS International
	American Association for the Advancement of Science
	Public Library of Science
	Medline
	PubMed
	Inspec
Mathematics	Springer publications
	American Mathematical Society
Humanities and	Project Muse

Subject	Journal source
social sciences	
Literature	American Comparative Literature Association
Philosophy	PhilPapers

Receive feedback on language, structure and layout

Professional editors proofread and edit your paper by focusing on:

- Academic style
- Vague sentences
- Grammar
- Style consistency

CREDIBLE NEWS SOURCES

More caution is required when considering using news articles (from newspapers and news sites), as the reliability of news sources available online varies significantly. Remember to apply the CRAAP test when evaluating news sources, focusing on purpose, authority and accuracy in particular.

Recommended credible news sources

News source	Main topics
The New York Times	News on business, politics and culture
The Wall Street Journal	News on general topics and business
The Washington Post	General news
BBC	General news
The Economist	World news and business
The New Yorker	Magazine featuring longer-form news and analysis

News source	Main topics
Reuters	News on politics and economy
Bloomberg	News on politics and economy
Foreign Affairs	A bi-monthly publication focused on international affairs
Politico	News on politics in the United States and Europe

The sources of information for research paper can be divided into many different ways. You can divide it on the basis of where to find the information, how to find the information and what kind of information to seek. Here we will look at where to find the information for a research paper.

Finding information for your research paper will not be an overwhelming process if you know where to look for the particular information. Once you know where to find the information you need to organize it in a sequential order. You need to devise a strategy because there are a wide array of sources available to seek information. In other words, you have to be selective about the sources that are available for your research. Once you decide what sources to use and where you can find them you need to make a sequential pattern. Decide how you will go through each of the sources you have selected for your study.

SOURCES OF INFORMATION FOR RESEARCH PAPER

The print on paper resources are the most basic and most important sources of information for your research. Libraries contain a wide array of information from where you can begin your research. If you are not sure about how to find information in the library ask the librarian as nobody knows more about the resources in a library then the librarian. There are many types of print resources other than the books.

Books are the most important source of information as we already discussed. Books contain information that is most authentic and well-researched source that you could rely upon. You can ask your research supervisor or your teacher how old a book you can use in your research.

Encyclopedias contain a wide array of information as they contain information on various subjects in alphabetical order. Some very basic information about a subject can easily be obtained from an encyclopedia, like definitions, types, forms, and history of any subject.

Bibliographies provide valuable insight on where to find information about your subject. Not sure what source will provide an information you can check the bibliographies and references section of your library.

You might find an unexpected source from the bibliography section that you never imagined.

Government publications are also an authentic source of information for your research. You can find statistical data about a subject matter in government records and a lot more information. The listings of the government publications is present in the libraries.

Dictionaries, maps, and atlases also carry valuable information that you can find in any library.

Non-print resources

Non-print resources can be any type of media that you can find in your library or through other sources like internet.

TV programs can be an important source of information especially in fields like history, geography, and media studies. Documentaries are valuable sources especially if you are sure about the authenticity of the narrative. TV programs and documentaries sometimes provide rare information that you may not be able to find anywhere else.

Videos in the form of tapes or discs are also available and you can check them in the media section of your library.

CDs, and audiotapes
Lectures and speeches
Interviews
Electronic resources

Today there is a wide range of electronic sources available for the research most of them are available online in the form of catalogs. Some of them are as follows:

Online catalogs provide you the listings of all type of electronic resources. You can check online books, periodicals, journals and newspaper listings. All libraries today have an online catalog of all the resources that are available online. Though libraries provide bibliographic cards as well as most libraries all books and journals are available online so online catalogs have taken the place of regular catalogs in many ways.

Internet websites are also valuable for research but you need to know the authenticity of the author and the content before you finalize that you can use this information in your research.

19
HOW TO DEFEND?

If you're about to complete, or have ever completed a graduate degree, you have most likely come across the term "thesis defense". In many countries, to finish a graduate degree, you have to write a thesis. In general, a thesis is a large paper based on a topic relating to your field of study. Once you hand in your thesis, you will be assigned a date to defend your work.

Your thesis defense meeting usually consists of you and a committee, consisting of two or more professors working in your program. It may also include other people, like professionals from other colleges or those who are working in your field. During your thesis defense, you will be asked questions about your work. The main purpose of your thesis defense is for the committee to make sure that you actually understand your field and focus area.

The questions are usually open-ended and require the student to think critically about their work. Note that at the time of your thesis defense, your paper has already been evaluated. The questions asked are not designed so that you actually have to aggressively "defend" your work, often your thesis defense is more of a formality required so that you can get your degree.

How long is a thesis defense?

How long your oral thesis defense is depends largely on the institution and requirements of your degree. It is best to consult your department or institution on this. In general, a thesis defense may take only 20 minutes, but it may also take two hours or more. This also depends on how much time is allocated to the presentation and questioning part. We will talk more about the different parts of a thesis defense below.

What happens at a thesis defense?

First of all, be aware that a thesis defense varies from country to country. This is just a general overview, but a thesis defense can take many different formats in different countries. Some are closed, other are public defenses. Some take place with two, some with more examiners. The same goes for the length of your thesis defense, as mentioned above. So the most important first step for you is to clarify with your department what the structure of your thesis defense will look like. In general, this is what happens at a thesis defense:

Your presentation

You might have to give a presentation, often with Powerpoint, Google slides or Keynote slides. Make sure to prepare an appropriate amount of slides. A general rule is to use about 10 slides for a 20-minute presentation. But that also depends on your specific topic and the way you present. The good news is, there will be plenty of time ahead of your thesis defense to prepare your slides and practice your presentation alone and in front of friends or family.

You can prepare your slides by using information from your thesis' first chapter (the overview of your thesis) as a framework or outline. Substantive information in your thesis should correspond with your slides. Make sure your slides are of good quality - both as regards the integrity of the information, and the appearance of your slides. If you need more help with how to prepare your presentation slides, both the ASQ Higher Education Brief and James Hayton have good guidelines on the topic.

Questions from the committee

As mentioned earlier, the committee will ask questions about your work after you finished your presentation. The questions will most likely be about the core content of your thesis, like what you learned from the study you conducted, but also why you chose your topic or how it will contribute to the existing body of knowledge. You might also be asked to summarize certain findings. Read your full thesis in preparation of the questions, so you know what you have written about.

While you are reading in preparation, you can create a list of possible questions and try to answer them. You can foresee many of the questions you will get by simply spending some time rereading your thesis. In addition, this blog post from researchClue.com lists 25 common thesis/project defense questions and how you may approach to answer them.

6 tips to help you prepare for your thesis defense
When you start your graduate degree, the end of it seems so far away. But then it ends up coming faster than you thought. You hand in your thesis, which was a lot of work, and as a last step before you officially receive your degree, you have to master your thesis defense. Here are a few tips on how to prepare for your thesis defense.

1. Anticipate questions and prepare for them

We've mentioned it before but you can really prepare for most of the questions you will be asked. Read through your thesis and while you're reading it, create a list of possible questions. In addition, as you will know who will be on the committee, look at the academic expertise of the committee members. In what areas would they most likely be focused? If possible, sit at other thesis defenses with these committee members to get a feeling for how they ask and what they ask. As a graduate student, you should generally be adept at anticipating test questions, so use this advantage to gather as much information as possible before your thesis defense meeting.

2. Dress for success

Your thesis defense is a formal event, often the entire department or university is invited to participate. It signals a critical rite of passage for graduate students and faculty who have supported them throughout a long and challenging process. While most universities don't have specific rules on how to dress for that event, do regard it with dignity and respect. This one might be a no-brainer, but know that you should dress as if you were on a job interview or delivering a paper at a conference.

3. Delegate

It might help you deal with your stress before your thesis defense to entrust someone with the smaller but important responsibilities of your thesis defense well ahead of schedule. This trusted person could be responsible for preparing the room of the day of defense, setting up equipment for the presentation or preparing and distributing handouts.

4. Have a backup plan

Technology is unpredictable. Life is too. There are no guarantees that your Powerpoint presentation will work at all or look the way it is supposed to do on the big screen. We've all been there. Make sure to have a plan B for these situations. Handouts can help when technology fails, or an additional fresh shirt for spilled coffee can save the day.

5. What to do when you don't know the answer

One of the scariest aspects of the defense is the possibility of being asked a question you can't answer. While you can prepare for some questions, you can never know exactly what the committee will ask. There will always be gaps in your knowledge. But your thesis defense is not about being perfect and knowing everything, it's about how you deal with challenging situations. You are not expected to know everything.

James Hayton writes on his blog that examiners will sometimes even ask questions they don't know the answer to, out of curiosity, or because they want to see how you think. While it is ok sometimes to just say "I don't know", he advises to try something like "I don't know, but I would think [...] because of x and y, but you would need to do [...] in order to find out". This shows that you have the ability to think as an academic.

6. Dealing with your nerves

You will be nervous. But the good news is - your examiners will expect you to be nervous. It is completely normal to be nervous. Being well prepared can help minimize your stress, but do know that your examiners have seen this many times before and are willing to help, by repeating questions for example if needed.

Two common symptoms of being nervous are talking really fast and nervous laughs. Try to slow yourself down, take a deep breath. Remember what feels like hours to you are just a few seconds in real life. Allow yourself to process the question, respond to it, and stop talking once you have responded. While a smile can often help dissolve a difficult situation, remember that nervous laughs can be irritating for your audience.

We all make mistakes and your thesis defense will most likely not be perfect. You are not expected to be perfect and the examiners already have plenty of experience with this and will guide you through it. Also remember that your thesis defense is often just a formality and the committee actually wants you to pass. If you are still nervous about your thesis defense, read this blog post by Dora Farkas at finishyourthesis.com. She debunks 5 common myths about thesis defenses and helps you see that your committee is not out to get you.

Frequently Asked Questions about preparing an excellent thesis defense
What should I wear for my thesis defense?

While most universities don't have specific rules on how to dress for that event, do regard it with dignity and respect. This one might be a no-brainer, but know that you should dress as if you were on a job interview or delivering a paper at a conference.

HOW CAN I DEAL WITH NERVES BEFORE MY THESIS DEFENSE?

It is completely normal to be nervous. Being well prepared can help minimize your stress, but do know that your examiners have seen this many times before and are willing to help, by repeating questions for example if needed. Slow yourself down, and take a deep breath.

What should I do if I can't answer a question during my thesis defense?

Your thesis defense is not about being perfect and knowing everything, it's about how you deal with challenging situations. James Hayton writes on his blog that it is ok sometimes to just say "I don't know", but he advises to try something like "I don't know, but I would think [...] because of x and y, you would need to do [...] in order to find out".

What should I do if technology fails me during my thesis defense?

Your Powerpoint presentation can get stuck or not look the way it is supposed to do on the big screen. It can happen and your supervisors know it. In general, handouts can always save the day when technology fails.

What are some tips to help me prepare for my thesis defense?

Here are a few tips on how to prepare for your thesis defense:

Anticipate questions and prepare for them
Dress for success
Delegate
Have a backup plan (in case technology fai

20
THE PERK AND PERILS OF RESEARCHING

15 Steps to Good Research

Judge the scope of the project.

Reevaluate the research question based on the nature and extent of information available and the parameters of the research project.

Select the most appropriate investigative methods (surveys, interviews, experiments) and research tools (periodical indexes, databases, websites).

Plan the research project.

Retrieve information using a variety of methods (draw on a repertoire of skills).

Refine the search strategy as necessary.
Write and organize useful notes and keep track of sources.

Use a citation manager: Zotero or Refworks

Evaluate sources using appropriate criteria.

Evaluating Internet Sources

Synthesize, analyze and integrate information sources and prior knowledge.

Revise hypothesis as necessary.

Use information effectively for a specific purpose.

Understand such issues as plagiarism, ownership of information (implications of copyright to some extent), and costs of information.

Cite properly and give credit for sources of ideas.

Use a citation manager: Zotero or Refworks

How to Improve Your Research Skills: 6 Research Tips

Research skills are a vital part of the writing process because they enable writers to find information and create an outline for their writing project—whether it's creative or academic writing. By developing organized and effective research methods, you'll be able to become knowledgeable in any field that you need to write about.

6 Tips for Improving Your Researching Skills

Here are a few research practices and tips to help you hone your research and writing skills:

1. **Start broad, then dive into the specifics**. Researching is a big task, so it can be overwhelming to know where to start—there's

nothing wrong with a basic internet search to get you started. Online resources like Google and Wikipedia, while not always accurate, are a great way to orient yourself in a topic, since they usually give a basic overview with a brief history and any key points.

2. **Learn how to recognize a quality source**. Not every source is reliable, so it's crucial that you can recognize the good sources from the not-so-good ones. To determine a reliable source, you'll need to use your analytical skills and critical thinking, and ask yourself the following questions: Does this source agree with other sources I have found? Is the author an expert in the field? Does the author's point of view have a conflict of interest regarding this topic?

3. **Verify information from several sources**. The internet is a big place, and, for the most part, anyone can say whatever they want online—many websites don't evaluate their content for factual accuracy. This means that there are plenty of unreliable resources out there, and even many that are outright incorrect. The best way to combat this is to make sure that whatever you find in your research, several different sources can verify that it is true. Rather than going off of one

webpage, make sure that at least two other places say something similar.

4. **Be open to surprising answers**. Good research is all about finding answers to your research questions—not necessarily as a way to verify what you already think you know. Solely looking for confirmation is a very limiting research strategy, since it involves picking and choosing what information to collect and prevents you from developing the most accurate understanding of the topic. When you conduct research, make sure to keep an open mind so that you can learn as deeply as possible.

5. **Stay organized**. During the data collection process, you'll be seeing a huge amount of information, from webpages to PDFs to videos. It's vital that you keep all of this information organized in some way to prevent yourself from losing something or not being able to cite something properly. There are plenty of ways to keep your research project organized, but here are a few common ones: Bookmarks in your Internet browser, index cards, and an annotated bibliography that you keep updated as you go.

6. **Take advantage of library resources**. If you still have questions about researching, don't worry—there are plenty of places out there to help you out, even if you're not a student doing academic or course-related research. In fact, many high school and university libraries offer resources not only for faculty members' and students' research but for the larger community. Be sure to check out library websites for research guides or access to specific databases.

The following steps outline a simple and effective strategy for writing a research paper. Depending on your familiarity with the topic and the challenges you encounter along the way, you may need to rearrange these steps.

Step 1: Identify and develop your topic

Selecting a topic can be the most challenging part of a research assignment. Since this is the very first step in writing a paper, it is vital that it be done correctly. Here are some tips for selecting a topic:

1. Select a topic within the parameters set by the assignment. Many times your instructor will give you clear guidelines as to what you can and cannot write about. Failure to work within these guidelines may result in your proposed paper being deemed unacceptable by your instructor.
2. Select a topic of personal interest to you and learn more about it. The research for and writing of a paper

will be more enjoyable if you are writing about something that you find interesting.

3. Select a topic for which you can find a manageable amount of information. Do a preliminary search of information sources to determine whether existing sources will meet your needs. If you find too much information, you may need to narrow your topic; if you find too little, you may need to broaden your topic.

4. Be original. Your instructor reads hundreds of research papers every year, and many of them are on the same topics (topics in the news at the time, controversial issues, subjects for which there is ample and easily accessed information). Stand out from your classmates by selecting an interesting and off-the-beaten-path topic.

5. Still can't come up with a topic to write about? See your instructor for advice.

Once you have identified your topic, it may help to state it as a question. For example, if you are interested in finding out about the epidemic of obesity in the American population, you might pose the question "What are the causes of obesity in America ?" By posing your subject as a question you can more easily identify the main concepts or keywords to be used in your research.

Step 2 : Do a preliminary search for information

Before beginning your research in earnest, do a preliminary search to determine whether there is enough information out there for your needs and to set the context of your research. Look up your keywords in the appropriate titles in the library's Reference collection (such as encyclopedias and dictionaries) and in other sources such as our catalog of books, periodical databases, and Internet search engines. Additional background information may be found in your lecture notes, textbooks, and reserve readings. You may find it necessary to adjust the focus of your topic in light of the resources available to you.

Step 3: Locate materials

With the direction of your research now clear to you, you can begin locating material on your topic. There are a number of places you can look for information:

If you are looking for books, do a subject search in the Alephcatalog. A Keyword search can be performed if the subject search doesn't yield enough information. Print or write down the citation information (author, title,etc.) and the location (call number and collection) of the item(s). Note the circulation status. When you locate the book on the shelf, look at the books located nearby; similar items are always shelved in the same area. The Aleph catalog also indexes the library's audio-visual holdings.

Use the library's **electronic periodical databases** to find magazine and newspaper articles. Choose the databases and formats best suited to your particular topic; ask at the librarian at the Reference Desk if you need help figuring out which database best meets your needs. Many of the articles in the databases are available in full-text format.

Use search engines (**Google**, **Yahoo**, etc.) and subject directories to locate materials on the Internet. Check the **Internet Resources** section of the Library web site for helpful subject links.

Step 4: Evaluate your sources

See the ***CARS Checklist for Information Quality*** for tips on evaluating the authority and quality of the information you have located. Your instructor expects that you will provide credible, truthful, and reliable information and you have every right to expect that the sources you use are providing the same. This step is especially important when using Internet resources, many of which are regarded as less than reliable.

Step 5: Make notes

Consult the resources you have chosen and note the information that will be useful in your paper. Be sure to document all the sources you consult, even if you there is a chance you may not use that particular source. The author, title, publisher, URL, and other information will be needed later when creating a bibliography.

Step 6: Write your paper

Begin by organizing the information you have collected. The next step is the rough draft, wherein you get your ideas on paper in an unfinished fashion. This step will help you organize your ideas and determine the form your final paper will take. After this, you will revise the draft as many times as you think necessary to create a final product to turn in to your instructor.

Step 7: Cite your sources properly

Give credit where credit is due; cite your sources.

Citing or documenting the sources used in your research serves two purposes: it gives proper credit to the authors of the materials used, and it allows those who are reading your work to duplicate your research and locate the sources that you have listed as references. The **MLA** and the **APA** Styles are two popular citation formats.

Failure to cite your sources properly is plagiarism. Plagiarism is avoidable!

Step 8: Proofread

The final step in the process is to proofread the paper you have created. Read through the text and check for any errors in spelling, grammar, and punctuation. Make sure the sources you used are cited properly. Make sure the message that you want to get across to the reader has been thoroughly stated.

Additional research tips:

- Work from the general to the specific -- find background information first, then use more specific sources.

- Don't forget print sources -- many times print materials are more easily accessed and every bit as helpful as online resources.
- The library has books on the topic of writing research papers at call number area LB 2369.
- If you have questions about the assignment, ask your instructor.
- If you have any questions about finding information in the library, ask the librarian.

21

MEAN, MEDIAN, MODE, AND RANGE

Mean, median, and mode are three kinds of "averages". There are many "averages" in statistics, but these are, I think, the three most common, and are certainly the three you are most likely to encounter in your pre-statistics courses, if the topic comes up at all.

The "mean" is the "average" you're used to, where you add up all the numbers and then divide by the number of numbers. The "median" is the "middle" value in the list of numbers. To find the median, your numbers have to be listed in numerical order from smallest to largest, so you may have to rewrite your list before you can find the median. The "mode" is the value that occurs most often. If no number in the list is repeated, then there is no mode for the list.

Mean, Median, Mode, and Range

The "range" of a list a numbers is just the difference between the largest and smallest values.

- **Find the mean, median, mode, and range for the following list of values:**

13, 18, 13, 14, 13, 16, 14, 21, 13

The mean is the usual average, so I'll add and then divide:

(13 + 18 + 13 + 14 + 13 + 16 + 14 + 21 + 13) ÷ 9 = 15

Note that the mean, in this case, isn't a value from the original list. This is a common result. You should not assume that your mean will be one of your original numbers.

The median is the middle value, so first I'll have to rewrite the list in numerical order:

13, 13, 13, 13, 14, 14, 16, 18, 21

There are nine numbers in the list, so the middle one will be the (9 + 1) ÷ 2 = 10 ÷ 2 = 5th number:

13, 13, 13, 13, 14, 14, 16, 18, 21

So the median is 14.

The mode is the number that is repeated more often than any other, so 13 is the mode.

The largest value in the list is 21, and the smallest is 13, so the range is 21 − 13 = 8.

mean: 15
median: 14
mode: 13
range: 8

Note: The formula for the place to find the median is "([the number of data points] + 1) ÷ 2", but you don't have to use this formula. You can just count in from both ends of the list until you meet in the middle, if you prefer, especially if your list is short. Either way will work.

Affiliate

- **Find the mean, median, mode, and range for the following list of values:**

  1, 2, 4, 7

The mean is the usual average:

$$(1 + 2 + 4 + 7) \div 4 = 14 \div 4 = 3.5$$

The median is the middle number. In this example, the numbers are already listed in numerical order, so I don't have to rewrite the list. But there is no "middle" number, because there are an even number of numbers. Because of this, the median of the list will be the mean (that is, the usual average) of the middle two values within the list. The middle two numbers are 2 and 4, so:

$$(2 + 4) \div 2 = 6 \div 2 = 3$$

So the median of this list is 3, a value that isn't in the list at all.

The mode is the number that is repeated most often, but all the numbers in this list appear only once, so there is no mode.

The largest value in the list is 7, the smallest is 1, and their difference is 6, so the range is 6.

mean: 3.5
median: 3
mode:none
range: 6

The values in the list above were all whole numbers, but the mean of the list was a decimal value. Getting a decimal value for the mean (or for the median, if you have an even number of data points) is perfectly okay; don't round your answers to try to match the format of the other numbers.

- **Find the mean, median, mode, and range for the following list of values:**

8, 9, 10, 10, 10, 11, 11, 11, 12, 13

The mean is the usual average, so I'll add up and then divide:

$$(8 + 9 + 10 + 10 + 10 + 11 + 11 + 11 + 12 + 13) \div 10 = 105 \div 10 = 10.5$$

The median is the middle value. In a list of ten values, that will be the $(10 + 1) \div 2 = 5.5$-th value; the formula is reminding me, with that "point-five", that I'll need to average the fifth and sixth numbers to find the median. The fifth and sixth numbers are the last 10 and the first 11, so:

$$(10 + 11) \div 2 = 21 \div 2 = 10.5$$

The mode is the number repeated most often. This list has two values that are repeated three times; namely, 10 and 11, each repeated three times.

The largest value is 13 and the smallest is 8, so the range is 13 − 8 = 5.

mean: 10.5
median: 10.5
modes: 10 and 11
range: 5

As you can see, it is possible for two of the averages (the mean and the median, in this case) to have the same value. But this is *not* usual, and you should *not* expect it.

Advertisement

Note: Depending on your text or your instructor, the above data set may be viewed as having no mode rather than having two modes, because no single solitary number was repeated more often than any other. I've seen books that go either way on this; there doesn't seem to be a consensus on the "right" definition of "mode" in the above case. So if you're not certain how you should answer the "mode" part of the above example, ask your instructor *before* the next test.

About the only hard part of finding the mean, median, and mode is keeping straight which "average" is which. Just remember the following:

mean: regular meaning of "average"
median: middle value
mode: most often

(In the above, I've used the term "average" rather casually. The technical definition of what we commonly refer to as the "average" is technically called "the arithmetic mean": adding up the values and then dividing by the number of values. Since you're probably more familiar with the concept of "average" than with "measure of central tendency", I used the more comfortable term.)

- **A student has gotten the following grades on his tests: 87, 95, 76, and 88. He wants an 85 or better overall. What is the minimum grade he must get on the last test in order to achieve that average?**

The minimum grade is what I need to find. To find the average of all his grades (the known ones, plus the unknown one), I have to add up all the grades, and then divide by the number of grades. Since I don't have a score for the last test yet, I'll use a variable to stand for this unknown value: "x". Then computation to find the desired average is:

$$(87 + 95 + 76 + 88 + x) \div 5 = 85$$

Multiplying through by 5 and simplifying, I get:

$$87 + 95 + 76 + 88 + x = 425$$

$$346 + x = 425$$

$$x = 79$$

He needs to get at least a 79 on the last test.

You can use the Mathway widget below to practice finding the median. Try the entered exercise, or type in your own exercise. Or try entering any list of numbers, and then selecting the option — mean, median, mode, etc — from what the widget offers you. Then click the button to compare your answer to Mathway's.

Please accept "preferences" cookies in order to enable this widget.

EPILOGUE

Long had Willy tell his notes to Jolly... until:

"Jolly, are you still there?"

"I cannot listen to your adventures further. I am quiet sleepy"

"Ok, I think I will go to the land on my own."

"Okay. Okay."

And the rest is history.

REFERENCES

https://www.questionpro.com/blog/what-is-research/

https://owlcation.com/academia/Why-Research-is-Important-Within-and-Beyond-the-Academe

https://theimportantsite.com/10-reasons-why-research-is-important/

https://www.reference.com/world-view/benefits-conducting-research-97226c9e6ac26d13

https://www.scribbr.com/methodology/types-of-research/

https://www.allassignmenthelp.com/blog/types-of-research/

https://www.infobloom.com/what-are-the-different-types-of-research.htm

https://www.scribbr.com/methodology/quantitative-research/

https://www.sciencedirect.com/topics/social-sciences/quantitative-research

https://www.sisinternational.com/what-is-quantitative-research/

https://www.scribbr.com/methodology/qualitative-research/

https://www.myperfectwords.com/blog/research-paper-guide/types-of-qualitative-research

http://adphealth.org/irtoolkit/research-methods-and-data-management/research-tools-and-techniques.html

https://leverageedu.com/blog/types-of-qualitative-research/

https://paperpile.com/g/thesis-defense/

https://libguides.merrimack.edu/research_help/Sources

https://www.scribbr.com/citing-sources/list-of-credible-sources-for-research/

http://readingcraze.com/index.php/sources-information-research-paper/

https://www.library.georgetown.edu/tutorials/research-guides/15-steps
https://www.masterclass.com/articles/how-to-improve-your-research-skills

https://www.nhcc.edu/student-resources/library/doinglibraryresearch/basic-steps-in-the-research-process
https://www.purplemath.com/modules/meanmode.htm

ABOUT THE AUTHOR

Wilmer Joel S. Decano, is a multi – awarded public school teacher, speaker, researcher and volunteer from Rizal, Philippines.

He is an Elementary Master Teacher at Exodus Elementary School, School Division of Rizal, Region 4-A CALABARZON of the Department of Education in the Philippines over sixteen years now.

He had been a demonstration teacher in various trainings and for a of different levels including District, Division, National and even International.

His expertise and dedication to craft also paved the way for him to become National Champion in teacher competition in Instructional Materials Development in the Least Mastered Skills in Science 6.

One of Wilmer's remarkable achievements was his first runner – up finish in GURONASYON's Search of Most Outstanding Elementary Teacher 2017. Since then, award and recognition as proofs of his excellent works as a teacher kept coming. Hewas a recipient of Gawad Pat National Award (2018), Gawad Panulat Awardee (2018), Natatanging Guro ng Bayan National Award (2018), Gawad Sikhay Awardee (2018).He is also conferred the Asian Achiever 2018 Awardee with highest distinction as Most Outstanding Educator and Red Cross Volunteer Advocate.

Beside his Extra Curricular activities, he also make sure that he always brings out his A-game in his teaching profession. He was adjudged as one of the Ten Inspiring Educators in the Philippines National Award (2019), Outstanding Master Teacher National Award (2019), Outstanding Volunteer National Award (2019), Gawad Sikhay Awardee National Award (2019). Innovative Teacher of the Year National Award (2019), Outstanding Writer of the Year National Award (2019), Outstanding Teacher of the Year National Award (2019). Excellence Award as Master Teacher (2020). National Excellence Award in Research (2020). National Excellence Award as Coach (2020). 2020 First Instabright National Awards Outstanding Teacher of the Year, Outstanding Writer of the Year and Innovative Teacher of the Year. Most Outstanding Master Teacher 2020. Gawad Ybarra Awardee 2020. He received International Recognition World Best Teacher Asian University International 2020. IQRA International Best Teacher Best Teacher 2020. Excellence Awards. Excellence in World

Literature Awards. Mahatma Gandhi Peace Prize Award.

He not only a teacher by profession he was also an active Red Cross Youth Adviser, He served with compassion and brought honor to his school with his excellent works. He produced 21 Most Outstanding Red Cross Youth and 24 Gawad Kabataan Awardee since he started being the adviser few years ago. Moreover, he also served Vice President Camarines Sur Educators Lions Club International. He was Vice President Visayas Lead Philippines.

As research advocate, it has been his advocacy to promote culture of research among schools in his division as means to develop the quality education in the country. In fact, he has initiated research capacity building for new researchers in the government.

As an educational leader, he had written a Modules for Science 6 in the Elementary level. He wrote some articles and books related to education which had been published in national and international journal and publications.

Wilmer holds a Bachelor's Degree in Elementary Education (BEEd) from the University of Luzon (Formerly Luzon Colleges). He had finished Academic Requirement leading to Master of Arts in Education (MaEd) Major in Educational Management from 2002. He was conferred by the Astrid Academy Sweden Humanitarian Doctorate Honoris Causa (DHum.). Then He received Social Work Honoris Causa (DSW) from United Nobles Rescue Services. Recently he received his Doctor of Literature and Arts (DLitt.) and Doctor of Philosophy in Peace Studies (DPhil.) at Theophany University Haiti. He was an Ambassador of Peace at Theophany University. Currently he was designated as Media Secretary International Human Rights Movement Philippines.